My
SPICED
KITCHEN

A *Middle Eastern* Cookbook

YANIV COHEN
The Spice Detective

PAGE STREET
PUBLISHING CO.

PAGE STREET
PUBLISHING CO.

First published in 2019 by
Page Street Publishing Co.
27 Congress Street, Suite 105
Salem, MA 01970
www.pagestreetpublishing.com

Distributed by Macmillan, sales in Canada by The Canadian Manda Group.

23 22 21 20 19   1 2 3 4 5

ISBN-13: 978-1-62414-707-4
ISBN-10: 1-62414-707-0

Library of Congress Control Number: 2018957261

Cover and book design by Rosie Stewart for Page Street Publishing Co.
Photography by Sonja Garnitschnig

Printed and bound in China

THIS IS A LOVE LETTER TO THE WOMEN IN MY FAMILY:

my mom, both my grandmothers and my many aunts. They put so much love and soul into their cooking and patiently showed me the way through their kitchens. I hope my sweet daughter, Rachel, will use this book as a guiding light to continue the spiced kitchen chain we are passing from one generation to the next . . .

CONTENTS

❧

INTRODUCTION
THE MAGNIFICENT WORLD OF SPICES

Food is a huge passion of mine, and I have always been especially drawn to the world of herbs and spices. My relatives used to tell me about the years when I was an infant and was placed in the kitchen in a bassinet while my mom cooked . . . and my mom cooked all the time! Our little apartment in Kiryat Malachi, in the southern district of Israel, always smelled of fresh garlic, cumin, paprika, coriander, caraway, cilantro and onions, so you can pretty much say I was born into the magnificent world of spices.

As the oldest of five boys, I was in charge of helping my mother cook and set the table. Growing up in Israel in a Sephardic Jewish family with North African and Middle Eastern roots, food was (and still is) an important part of our culture. Every Shabbat and holiday had its unique set of incredible dishes—each one beautifully seasoned. I was always enthralled with the colors, scents, origins and properties of those spices. Nothing worth eating could be cooked without the help of a spice or two.

However, there is one spice that molded me into The Spice Detective: turmeric. People joke about how much I love this spice, but turmeric is where it all began for me. When I was eight years old, I fell on a piece of glass while playing with some friends and badly cut my hand. As the blood gushed out, I started panicking. One of our neighbors saw what happened while hanging laundry outside to dry, and she told me not to move. A few moments later, she showed up with a canister of powdered turmeric and began placing handfuls of it on the wound. To my astonishment, my hand stopped bleeding. That encounter is the inspiration behind this book and continues to fuel my love of spices to this day.

As I began to delve into the world of culinary herbs and spices as a young adult, I became fascinated with the medicinal properties of food. Throughout history, many cultures have used herbs, plants and spices to treat different health conditions. But, I had no idea that not every family or culture was as connected to the world of spices as I was. I took it for granted. When I moved to the United States, I realized that the knowledge and splendor of spices were not known to many, and I quickly took it upon myself to share what I learned with my American friends. The dishes, the flavors and the health benefits were always good topics of conversation at the dinner table. It was the birth of my daughter, Rachel, that inspired me to share the healing properties of spices and my passion for cooking with a larger audience. It was then that The Spice Detective became a reality.

My goal is to introduce you to the incredible flavors, aromas, properties and health benefits of Middle Eastern spices and herbs, while showing you how to incorporate them into everyday dishes that will delight all your senses.

Have you ever wondered why the steamiest and most tropical regions of the world (India, North and Central Africa, and Thailand, for example) have some of the richest and spiciest dishes, while colder climates, such as Northern Europe, don't? The answer is simple. In hotter regions, spices help preserve dishes longer, and the antiseptic properties in some of those spices inhibit bacterial growth.

SPICES AROUND THE WORLD: BODY, MIND AND SOUL

So, what are spices exactly? They are seeds, fruit, roots, bark or other plant substances primarily used for flavoring, coloring or preserving food. Herbs are the leaves, flowers or stems of plants used for flavoring or garnishing. Many spices and herbs have antimicrobial properties and are also used in medicine, religious rituals, cosmetics and perfumes.

The history of herbs and spices is just as interesting as their properties. In fact, human history is integrally intertwined with food as medicine, and we have learned so much about different cultures simply from their cuisines and rituals. The earliest documentation of spices and herbs was in ancient times, when hunter-gatherers wrapped meat in the leaves of bushes, and by chance, realized that this actually enriched the taste of the meats. A love of spices and herbs grew around the world as time passed, with more and more people using them for medicinal purposes, flavor agents and commercial trade. For example, in 1000 BC, the Bible mentions that Queen Sheba visited King Solomon in Jerusalem and offered him "120 measures of gold, many spices, and precious stones." This precious commodity was valued differently throughout the ages . . . but it was always valued.

ANCIENT EGYPT: WELLNESS

Records show that laborers who built the Great Pyramid of Giza consumed onions and fresh garlic as a way to boost wellness, and Cleopatra, herself, thought nigella seeds could cure anything but death.

EARLY CHINESE INFLUENCE: BREATH MINTS

Exported from Moluccas (the Spice Islands), cloves were among the many herbs beloved by Chinese royalty, not for their taste, but for their scent. Anecdotal evidence suggests that Chinese courtiers during the third century BC sucked on these tiny cloves to enhance the smell of their breath when addressing the emperor. In fact, before even reaching his highness's royal quarters, courtiers were presented with a clove by palace servants.

ANCIENT MESOPOTAMIA: HERBAL OILS

The world's first vegetable oil was created by the ancient Assyrians, who used sesame. They also made olive oil, pistachio oil and laurel berry oil. It's been said that these handmade products were traded along the Silk Road at the time of Jesus's birth. We're still making these oils today!

INDIAN ORIGINS: HERBAL HEALING

Indians have been using black pepper, cinnamon, turmeric and cardamom since the beginning of time, and although they valued them as culinary condiments, what they really saw as beneficial was their ability to heal. The ancient Indian surgeon Susruta even placed white mustard and other aromatic plants in patients' bedsheets to ward off evil spirits.

GREECE AND ROME: MEDICAL SCIENCE AND SCENTED BALMS

Hippocrates writes about spices—saffron, cinnamon, thyme, coriander, mint and marjoram—identifying potential herbal remedies. And of these remedies (400, to be exact) about half are still used today. In the first century AD, Dioscorides, a Greek physician, wrote *De Materia Medica*, a book cataloguing herbal remedies. These writings were referenced in both the East and West for over 1,500 years to study medicine and botany.

However, the Romans are a different story. They saw spices and herbs as ways to heighten their already extravagant lifestyle. For example, after taking a bath, it was popular for Romans to use spices and scented balms. And who can blame them? Spice aromas can act as stimulants and aphrodisiacs.

ARABIA: THE SPICE TRADE

In the ancient Arab and Muslim world, spices and herbs were commercially traded and largely exported from Arabia. Most popular to traders were cassia and cinnamon, and to create a monopoly over the spice trade, Arabians kept the source of their products a great secret, spinning fantastical tales of how they attained them, in order to keep their market value high. It took the ancient Roman scholar Pliny to finally make the connection between Arabian tales and the inflated price of these spices.

EUROPE: SPICE GARDENS

According to legend, the first person to plant a garden of herbs was Charlemagne, king of France and emperor of the West. This ignited a trend to cultivate culinary herbs such as anise, fennel, fenugreek, sage, thyme, parsley and coriander, paving a new path for gastronomic fashion that would create flavors never before experienced. No wonder French cuisine is one of the most celebrated in the world!

AGE OF SPICE DISCOVERY: MARCO POLO

Marco Polo, journeying the globe from 1271 to 1295, frequently wrote about the sumptuous and never-before-tasted spices he encountered in the different regions he explored. Sesame oil in Afghanistan, ginger in the city of Peking and 10,000 pounds of pepper delivered each day in Hangchow. And although there's suggestions that his writings initially fueled the spice trade, it wasn't until Christopher Columbus that the spice trade exploded.

AMERICAN HISTORY: HERBAL TEA

The archetypal drink of Great Britain was tea. Prim and posh, this afternoon beverage, most often served with mini tea sandwiches, scones and cakes, has been a pastime of English culture since the seventeenth century. With tea's arrival in the American colonies, it only seemed fitting that the colonists would pick up this dashing and dainty habit too. However, the long cherished career of high tea took a turn for the worse during the American Revolution, with colonists calling it unpatriotic and unfitting for American social etiquette.

It was then that spices and herbs became a replacement, with tea drinkers sipping on hot water dipped with sassafras bark, chamomile flowers, spearmint leaves, lemon balm leaves and raspberry leaves instead.

TWENTY-FIRST CENTURY: GLOBAL SPICE MARKET AND THE INTERNET

Today, more and more chefs are experimenting and incorporating exotic spices into their creations. Unlike earlier times when monopolies dominated the spice trade, commerce in spices is now relatively decentralized. The world is a global spice market, each country specializing in its own production of herbs, creating their own dishes and elevating their own flavor palates.

With the global reach of the Internet, chefs like myself can share their love for spices on social media. Furthermore, the interest in spices and herbs as flavor agents and medicinal properties is continuing to grow among the masses. As research progresses, scientists are finding truth in the observations of our ancestors, and we are coming full circle.

THE SPICE DETECTIVE'S TIPS FOR COOKING AND USING SPICES

In this book, I'll introduce you to some of my favorite spices and spice mixes that I grew up with. Some will be familiar to you and some may be new. I encourage you to try, smell, touch and taste them all. In each chapter, organized by spice, I include several of my favorite recipes. They are easy to follow and yield wonderful and flavorful dishes. I observe kosher practices, so I don't mix dairy and meat. I also don't cook with pork or shellfish.

Before starting this journey, here are some tips from my kitchen to yours:

1. In many markets, you'll find sacks of open spices igniting your senses and calling your name. Although it is an attractive look, opened spices often lose their flavor and aroma. If you buy spices at the market, feel free to ask for a sample. Smell, taste and feel the power of the spice. Stale spice will not be potent and powerful, so don't buy it. Choose high-quality, organic, closed packages of spices with an expiration date on the package.

2. Make sure the store has its spices in a cool, dark aisle away from windows where the spices won't be exposed to the sun and heat.

3. Buy smaller quantities so you don't have to store spices in your kitchen for a long time, as they lose their freshness and properties over time.

4. The women in my family always stored spices in the refrigerator or freezer. The cool temperature helps keep the spices fresher longer.

5. Read the labels. Make sure there are no additives or MSG added. When possible, find your spices from a reputable, organic source. Some commercial sources mix their spices with flour and other additives.

6. If you're new to a specific spice, get to know it. Smell and taste it. Understand the flavor and aroma of each spice, and use your discretion when it comes to quantities. Add a little at a time just like you add salt and pepper. Many spices are considered an acquired taste. Give yourself and your family time to appreciate the flavors.

7. Spices with strong colors, such as paprika and turmeric, should be added early in the cooking process. Spices that are rich in flavor, such as cumin, caraway seeds and coriander, can be added toward the end. Spices that are herbal or derived from fruit, such as sumac and za'atar, don't have to cook at all and are often sprinkled on top of your dish or salad for extra flavor and garnish.

8. In each recipe, my salt of choice is Celtic salt. This page is too short to name the health benefits of this amazing unprocessed salt. Use it if you can.

9. Although each chapter is dedicated to one spice, many recipes combine a few spices together as they fortify each other's aroma and flavors.

10. I highly recommend splurging on a spice grinder. Grind your own spices when possible. It's easy and will preserve the flavors, freshness and mineral oils of spices and herbs.

I hope you will become familiar with these spices, fall in love with them and learn new ways to incorporate them into your kitchen. Let these recipes inspire you to further explore the magnificent world of spices.

ALLSPICE

This aromatic herb brings the smell of cinnamon, nutmeg and clove to life. Allspice, a seasoning most commonly used in Caribbean dishes, is derived from the dried fruits of the allspice tree, better known as the evergreen shrub or Pimenta dioica. Native to the Greater Antilles, South America, Central America and Jamaica, this fragrant shrub grows green berries, each of which contains two seeds that are a bit larger than peppercorns.

The first European to encounter these dark-colored seeds was Christopher Columbus, while on the island of Jamaica during his second voyage to the New World. Commissioned to bring back spices for King Ferdinand and Queen Isabella of Spain, it's no surprise that Columbus and his explorers were mystified by these sun-dried seeds. But this spice didn't get its name until the seventeenth century, when the British dubbed it allspice for its all-encompassing perfume. They couldn't quite put a finger on what these savory seeds reminded them of, as their fragrance evoked multiple spices. Despite its name, however, allspice is its own entity.

A combination of flavors including juniper, peppercorn, cinnamon, nutmeg and clove, allspice is the ideal one-stop-shop ingredient for savory dishes. Because of its Jamaican roots, allspice is now the most prominent cooking agent in Caribbean and Latin cuisine, most notably in Jamaican jerk seasoning.

Moreover, what's even more special about these little balls of flavor, is their medicinal properties. Allspice can be used to alleviate the effects of indigestion, abdominal pain, menstrual cramps and colds. One of its main chemical properties, known as eugenol, is used by dentists to eliminate bacteria in the teeth and gums, and it's even used to flavor toothpaste. Most impressive are the high levels of potassium, known for preventing strokes and heart attacks, among other benefits.

If you're looking for a spice to have on hand as a two-in-one cooking and medicinal ingredient, look no further. With its warm flavors, it will complement all of your savory and sweet dishes.

Spice up your morning with these delicious, tender muffins. Allspice is a perfect companion for your morning joe and will surely give you a boost of energy as you start your day. Take a few muffins to the office and your coworkers will be grateful!

ALLSPICE COCONUT BREAKFAST MUFFINS

YIELD: 24 MUFFINS

1½ cups (190 g) all-purpose flour

1½ cups (141 g) oat bran

1 tsp baking soda

½ cup (38 g) coconut flakes

1 tsp ground allspice

¼ tsp kosher salt

½ cup (113 g) unsalted butter, at room temperature

⅓ cup (65 g) packed brown sugar

2 eggs

1 cup (240 g) sour cream

⅓ cup (115 g) silan (date syrup)

1 cup (140 g) dried currants (or diced dates)

Preheat the oven to 350°F (175°C). Line two muffin tins with paper liners.

In a large bowl, combine the flour, oat bran, baking soda, coconut, allspice and salt. Set aside.

Use an electric mixer to beat the butter and brown sugar together until smooth. Add the eggs and beat to combine. Add the sour cream and silan and continue beating to combine. Slowly add the flour mixture, mixing until incorporated. Once smooth, fold in the currants.

Spoon the batter into the prepared muffin tin. Place in the oven and bake for 20 to 30 minutes, or until a knife inserted into the center of a muffin comes out clean and dry.

CHEF'S TIP: Add ½ teaspoon of cardamom for an extra morning kick.

This "soupy" stew is seasoned with allspice along with some help from cumin and turmeric, creating a lovely, hearty, aromatic soup for the fish lovers in your family. You can also use a whole fish cut into chunks and substitute the salmon and halibut with cod, snapper, bass or a mix-and-match of your favorite fish.

ALLSPICE FISH STEW

YIELD: 6 SERVINGS

4 tbsp (60 ml) extra-virgin olive oil

1 large onion, chopped

4 celery ribs, chopped

2 medium carrots, chopped

6 cloves garlic, slivered

4 tomatoes, chopped

½ tsp ground allspice

½ tsp cumin

½ tsp turmeric

4 cups (1 L) water

Salt and pepper, to taste

½ tsp sugar (optional)

1 lb (450 g) salmon, cut into 2" (5-cm) cubes

1 lb (450 g) halibut, cut into 2" (5-cm) cubes

½ bunch cilantro or parsley, chopped

Heat the olive oil in a large soup pot or Dutch oven over medium heat. Add the onion, celery and carrots and sauté for 10 minutes, or until the onion is tender. Add the garlic and cook for a few more minutes, or until the garlic is golden and fragrant. Be careful not to burn the garlic. Add the tomatoes, allspice, cumin and turmeric and continue to cook, stirring often, until the tomatoes soften, about 15 minutes.

Add the water, salt and pepper. Reduce the heat to low and simmer for 15 to 20 minutes. Adjust the seasonings, if necessary. If the stew tastes too acidic, add the sugar to balance the flavors.

Season the fish with salt and pepper and place in the soup. Simmer for 15 minutes, or until the fish is cooked through and flakes easily.

Remove the soup from the heat and stir in the cilantro or parsley. Let the soup rest, covered, for 10 to 15 minutes to blend the flavors before serving.

CHEF'S TIP: This soup is awesome with thick, crusty country bread. Mix some olive oil with a little crushed garlic, brush the bread slices on both sides with the oil and garlic mix and grill for a few minutes on each side.

This is a fragrant stew that's simple to make and fun to experiment with. For example, I love adding peas and carrots for color, flavor and nutrition, just like my mom used to do. You can add cauliflower florets, potatoes, sweet potatoes or even mushrooms. Additionally, you can adjust how much water you use to make this stew extra saucy or thick. Serve over couscous, rice or quinoa.

ALLSPICE AND GINGER CHICKEN STEW

YIELD: 6–8 SERVINGS

4 tbsp (60 ml) extra-virgin olive oil

1 medium onion, chopped

8 boneless, skinless chicken thighs (5–6 oz [140–168 g] each)

2 tsp (4 g) ground allspice

1 tsp grated ginger

1 tsp sweet paprika

5 tomatoes, chopped

3 cups (700 ml) water

3 carrots, peeled and cut into ½" (13-mm) slices

2 cups (290 g) sweet peas, fresh or frozen

2–3 thyme sprigs

½ tsp brown sugar

Salt and pepper, to taste

In a large saucepan, heat the olive oil over medium-high heat and add the onion. Sauté for 10 minutes, or until the onion is golden. Add the chicken thighs and brown lightly on each side, approximately 7 minutes. You may need to do this in batches to avoid crowding the pan.

Add the allspice, ginger, paprika and chopped tomatoes and simmer for a few minutes. Add the water, carrots, peas, thyme sprigs, brown sugar, salt and pepper. Adjust the seasonings to taste. Let it simmer for 30 minutes, or until the carrots are soft but not falling apart.

CHEF'S TIP: I don't use chicken breasts for stews as they tend to get very dry. Always look for thighs, which remain tender and moist even when slightly overcooked.

I learned to explore the many possibilities of pasta sauce while visiting Venice for a few months when I was 21. My friends were eager to teach me as I showcased my Israeli flavors. My family never used sage, and once I tried it in Italy, I was hooked! I was also surprised when I tried pumpkin sauce. Who knew!? The allspice in this recipe complements the sage and pumpkin, creating a unique flavor.

ALLSPICE-SCENTED PUMPKIN, SAGE AND ALMOND FUSILLI

YIELD: 6 SERVINGS

1 (16-oz [450-g]) box fusilli pasta (or your favorite dry pasta)

¼ cup (55 g) unsalted butter

1 medium onion, chopped

4 cloves garlic, slivered

1 (15-oz [425-g]) can pumpkin or squash purée

½ tsp ground allspice

½ cup (120 g) mascarpone cheese

¼ cup (25 g) freshly grated Parmigiano-Reggiano cheese, plus more for garnishing

12 leaves fresh sage

Salt and pepper, to taste

½ cup (50 g) sliced almonds

Chives, chopped (optional)

Cook the pasta until al dente according to the package directions. Set aside.

Melt the butter in a large saucepan over medium-low heat. Add the onion and cook until golden, about 5 minutes. Add the garlic and sauté for a few more minutes. Don't overcook the garlic. Mix in the pumpkin purée, allspice, mascarpone cheese, Parmigiano-Reggiano cheese and the sage.

Turn off the heat. Add the pasta and toss to coat thoroughly. Season with salt and pepper, to taste.

Transfer the pasta to a serving bowl or individual plates. Sprinkle with the almonds, chives (if desired) and a little more Parmigiano-Reggiano and serve hot.

CHEF'S TIP: For extra crunch, toast the almonds in a hot skillet for a few minutes, or until lightly browned.

This is one of my favorite healthy desserts. Using apple juice instead of white sugar, it's almost like an elixir of sorts infused with the goodness of those spices and dried fruit and pear. A ½ cup (120 g) of brown sugar is optional—only if you like it sweeter. The apple juice makes it sweet enough for me. If you really want to turn this into a treat, top with vanilla ice cream, whipped cream or Gorgonzola cheese.

MIDDLE EASTERN ALLSPICE POACHED PEARS

YIELD: 6 SERVINGS

4 cups (1 L) apple juice, plus more if necessary for poaching

4 cups (1 L) red wine

2 tbsp (30 ml) lemon juice

1 tbsp (6 g) whole allspice

6 cinnamon sticks

6 whole star anise

1 tsp ground cardamom

6 large, firm pears, peeled with stalks attached

3 cups (480 g) dried fruit, such as prunes, apricots, dried apples or raisins

In a medium saucepot, combine the apple juice, red wine, lemon juice, allspice, cinnamon sticks, star anise and cardamom, and bring to a gentle boil over medium-low heat for 20 to 25 minutes, or until the sauce and spices are fully incorporated and fragrant. Reduce the heat and simmer gently for 5 minutes. This will allow the spices to infuse into the liquids.

Cut the bottom of each pear so they can sit flat. Place the pears in the pot covered in liquid. Add more apple juice if necessary. Poach over low heat for 15 to 20 minutes, or until tender but not soft. Make sure the pears are still slightly firm so they don't fall apart when serving.

Remove the pears from the pot, and while they cool off, add the dried fruit medley to the spiced sauce. Simmer for 20 minutes, or until the liquid reduces and becomes syrupy.

Pour a small amount of the syrup in the bottom of six dessert dishes, and place the pears on top. Add the dried fruit medley to the plate around each pear. Garnish with the cinnamon sticks and star anise and drizzle more syrup on top of the pear.

CHEF'S TIP: If you want a light-colored dessert, use white wine instead of the red!

ANISE

Despite the similarities of name and flavor, anise and star anise are two very different spices. True anise, which is what we like to use in the Middle East, is an herb in the parsley family that produces small seeds with a potent, licorice-like flavor. Star anise is the star-shaped fruit of a tree that's native to warm-climate areas of China and Indochina. The unrelated plants contain the same flavor profile, but they are used in two different regions.

Found in ancient Egypt and eventually transported to the Mediterranean and Europe, the anise plant has been delivering a licorice spice to taste palettes since at least 1500 BC. The Romans, the mathematician Pythagoras, Hippocrates and Dioscorides also valued anise for its medicinal uses and its culinary delights. Between using the anise seed as a cough and digestive aid and adding it as an ingredient in wedding cakes, the ancient Romans found every way to extract its benefits.

In fact, the story goes that the first wedding cake ever to be baked was one flavored with anise, and this tradition of using anise as a sweetening agent was passed on for centuries. The main ingredient in licorice, the anise seed's ability to bring Candy Land to life is extraordinary. Savory plates like Italian sausage, braised duck (page 32) and roasted fennel (page 27) are elevated by its touch. It's even the main ingredient in spirits—including Greece's ouzo, Italy's sambuca and France's Pernod. Pound cakes, Italian biscotti and biscuits are a no-go without it.

Fennel is underutilized in the American kitchen, and it's a shame. It has such a unique flavor that adds great depth to dishes and salads. I love fennel raw, cooked, roasted . . . you name it! I also love liquor made from it as it is a wonderful palate cleanser and digestion aid. Adding anise to fennel brings its flavor out front and center. This is great served as a side dish.

ANISE-ROASTED FENNEL

YIELD: 8 SERVINGS

4 whole large fennel bulbs, cut into quarters

4 tbsp (60 ml) extra-virgin olive oil

Zest of 1 lemon

1 tsp whole anise seeds

Salt and pepper, to taste

8 thyme sprigs

2 tbsp (30 ml) balsamic vinegar reduction (can be reduced at home or bought in the gourmet section of many grocery stores)

Preheat the oven to 375°F (190°C).

Place the fennel on a lightly oiled roasting pan. Drizzle the olive oil over the fennel. Sprinkle the fennel with the lemon zest, anise seeds, salt and pepper and place the thyme sprigs in between. Roast uncovered for 20 to 25 minutes, or until tender.

Serve the fennel on a tray and drizzle with the balsamic vinegar reduction.

This is the soup my mom used to make in the dead of winter. Even though it never snowed in our hometown, there would be days of cold, winter rain. For us, growing up in a warm country, this was reason enough to stay home. My mom worried we would get wet and then get sick, so we were snowed in without the snow. This North African–inspired semolina soup is thick, fragrant, warm and oh, so comforting.

ANISE-SCENTED SEMOLINA SOUP

YIELD: 10 SERVINGS

2 tbsp (30 ml) plus ⅓ cup (80 ml) extra-virgin olive oil, divided

1 medium-large onion, diced

3 qt (3 L) water

6 cloves garlic, slivered

½ tsp ground anise

3 celery stalks, diced

Salt and pepper, to taste

1½ cups (240 g) coarse semolina

Cilantro leaves, for garnishing

Whole anise, for garnishing

In a large soup pot, heat 2 tablespoons (30 ml) of the olive oil over medium heat. Add the diced onion, and sauté for 10 to 12 minutes, or until translucent. Pour in the water and bring it to a boil. Add the garlic, anise, celery, remaining ⅓ cup (80 ml) of olive oil, salt and pepper. Cook for 30 minutes, or until the celery is tender.

Reduce the heat to medium-low and stir in the semolina, pouring it gradually while stirring in order to prevent clumping. Cover and cook for 10 minutes, or until the semolina is cooked. Adjust the seasonings. Garnish with the cilantro and a few whole anise seeds and serve hot.

CHEF'S TIP: For a richer, more-chicken flavored soup, use chicken bouillon instead of salt!

These cookies are perfect with coffee or tea. They are crispy and aromatic and will store well in an airtight container on your kitchen counter for about a week.

ANISETTE COOKIES

YIELD: APPROXIMATELY 40 COOKIES

1 cup (220 g) unsalted butter, at room temperature

¾ cup (170 g) packed brown sugar

2 tsp (4 g) whole anise seeds

Zest of 1 orange

1 cup (140 g) dried currants or raisins

3 eggs

3 cups (375 g) all-purpose flour

1 tbsp (8 g) baking powder

¼ tsp salt

1 cup (120 g) powdered sugar

Preheat the oven to 350°F (175°C). Line a baking sheet with parchment paper.

In a large bowl, beat together the butter and brown sugar. Add the anise seeds, orange zest, currants and eggs and mix together. Add the flour, baking powder and salt and keep mixing to create a dough. The dough won't be too smooth, but it shouldn't fall apart as you form the cookies.

Roll the dough in small batches. Use a cookie cutter to form your favorite cookie shape.

Place the cookies on the baking sheet and bake for 15 minutes, or until the cookies are golden and a toothpick inserted into the center of a cookie comes out clean and dry.

Cool for at least 20 minutes and dust with the powdered sugar.

If you're a duck lover and you simply live for spices as I do, this delicious recipe will satisfy all of your senses. Duck really comes alive when you add a little sweetness to balance its rich, gamy qualities, and it pairs so well with the aroma of anise, orange and prunes! If you're not a fan of duck, you can try the same recipe with chicken.

DUCK LEG BRAISED WITH ANISE, ORANGE AND PRUNES

YIELD: 4 SERVINGS

4 duck legs, about ½ lb (230 g) each

Salt and pepper, to taste

3 tbsp (45 ml) extra-virgin olive oil

1 onion, chopped

4 cloves garlic, slivered

3 tbsp (45 ml) orange-flavored liqueur, such as Grand Marnier (optional)

¼ cup (55 g) packed brown sugar

3 cinnamon sticks

1 tsp whole anise seeds

1 tsp anise powder

2 cups (475 ml) water

1 cup (180 g) pitted prunes

1 cup (240 ml) orange juice

1 orange peel, cut into strips

Chopped cilantro, parsley, chervil, mint or a combination, to taste

Season the duck on all sides with salt and pepper.

In a large, heavy pot or Dutch oven, heat the olive oil over medium-high heat. Once the oil is hot, sear the duck on both sides for 10 to 12 minutes or until golden brown. Remove the legs from the oil and set aside.

Drain half of the fat from the pot and brown the onion in the remaining fat until the onion is translucent, about 6 minutes. Add the garlic and cook for 2 minutes.

Add the orange-flavored liqueur, if using. Reduce the heat to low and add the sugar, cinnamon and anise seeds and powder, stirring until the sugar dissolves. Add the water, prunes, orange juice and peel. Stir well, bring to a boil and then reduce the heat. Return the duck to the pot.

Cover the pot and simmer with the duck partially covered by the sauce for about 2 hours, or until the duck is very tender and the sauce is reduced by about half.

Place the duck legs on a serving plate drizzled with the sauce and top with the cilantro, parsley, chervil and/or mint.

CHEF'S TIP: If the sauce hasn't reduced enough but the duck is perfectly tender, remove the duck and continue to reduce the sauce.

I credit this recipe to the Tunisian side of my family, especially Grandma Margaret the Great. These little meatballs are soaked with harissa and spices. The flavor is similar to merguez, which are Moroccan lamb sausages. I remember being in awe and bliss as I dipped the challah bread in this sauce and bit into these meatballs. I find it funny how a simple dish can bring so much happiness! Serve with fresh bread.

GRANDMA MARGARET'S ANISE AND HARISSA MEATBALLS

YIELD: 20 SMALL MEATBALLS

FOR THE MEATBALLS

1 lb (450 g) ground beef or lamb

6 cloves garlic, minced

1 tsp ground caraway seeds

½ tsp ground anise seeds

½ tsp cumin

1 tbsp (5 g) Harissa with Caraway, Cumin and Coriander (page 56) or (15 g) tomato paste

2 tbsp (30 ml) extra-virgin olive oil

Salt and pepper, to taste

FOR THE SAUCE

3 cups (700 ml) water

2 tbsp (10 g) Harissa with Caraway, Cumin and Coriander (page 56) or (30 g) tomato paste

4 cloves garlic, slivered

1 tsp ground caraway seeds

½ tsp cumin

4 tbsp (60 ml) extra-virgin olive oil

Salt and pepper, to taste

To make the meatballs, in a medium bowl, mix the ground beef, garlic, caraway, anise, cumin, harissa, olive oil, salt and pepper, and work the mixture with your hands to fully incorporate the ingredients. Set the mixture aside.

To make the sauce, add the water to a small pot over medium heat. Add the harissa and mix well. Add the garlic, caraway, cumin, olive oil, salt and pepper, and stir as you bring the sauce to simmer. Reduce the heat and adjust the seasoning.

Make 1½-inch (3.8-cm)-diameter meatballs and drop them into the sauce.

Let the meatballs cook for about 15 minutes, or until cooked through. Remove from the heat and let them sit for 15 minutes before serving.

You can find Turkish bourekas on every corner of Tel Aviv, and we love them! What's not to love about crunchy flaky filo dough filled with melting goodness? Assorted cheeses, spinach, onion, potatoes or meat all work for the right customer. Usually served with hard-boiled eggs and pickles, I vary my own spiced version depending on the mood or guests. I stuffed the bourekas in this recipe with onions, spinach, goat cheese and anise seed. If you serve them with a side of ouzo, you'll feel like you're in Greece.

ONION, SPINACH, ANISE AND GOAT CHEESE BOUREKAS

YIELD: 4 BOUREKAS

3 tbsp (45 ml) extra-virgin olive oil, plus more for coating the baking sheet

2 medium Spanish onions, diced

3 cloves garlic, minced

1 (9-oz [255-g]) box frozen spinach, thawed

1 tsp paprika

½ tsp anise powder

Salt and pepper, to taste

2 tbsp (34 g) goat cheese

½ cup (70 g) all-purpose flour

4 squares (4" x 4" [10.2 x 10.2 cm]) frozen filo dough, thawed

2 tbsp (30 ml) water

1 egg

Whole anise seeds, as desired

Preheat the oven to 350°F (175°C) and coat a baking sheet with olive oil.

In a large saucepan, heat the olive oil over medium heat and sauté the onions for 10 to 12 minutes, or until golden brown. Add the garlic and sauté for 1 to 2 minutes.

Squeeze any excess liquid from the spinach and add it to the pan. Sauté for 10 minutes, and then add the paprika, anise powder, salt and pepper. Remove from the heat and let the mixture cool off a bit, and then fold in the goat cheese. Adjust the seasonings.

Flour a flat surface and place the dough squares on it. Place approximately 1½ tablespoons (22 g) of the mixture in the center of each square and fold the squares over to form triangles. Seal the edges tightly together with a little oil and press.

In a small bowl, whisk together the water and egg. Brush the bourekas with the egg mixture. Sprinkle the anise seeds over them, as desired. Bake for 25 to 30 minutes or until crispy and brown.

CHEF'S TIP: Serve with hard-boiled eggs, pickles, olives and Cumin Cardamom Yemenite S'chug (page 114).

BAHARAT

Baharat is the Arabic word for "spices," and is a spice blend used in Middle Eastern cuisine. This mixture of finely ground aromatic herbs is often used to season ground beef, lamb, chicken and soups and may even be used as a condiment.

My mom always kept it in stock as it is very widely used in Iraqi cuisine, and our kibbeh dishes were always filled with meat seasoned with baharat. Between inventive tones of sweet-meets-spicy and a last-minute rush of heat, this spice mix is reminiscent of the lingering sunsets during our family picnic beach days and the warm sun resting underneath the mesmerizing Mediterranean sky.

The beauty of this blend is in the perfectly combined aromas and herbs—a one-stop-shop spice bag that unites black pepper, cardamom, cinnamon, nutmeg and more. With baharat, there's no need to fret about adding any other seasoning to your recipe. It's all right here!

Baharat is one of the most important spice mixtures in Jewish Iraqi cuisine, and I remember as a child that each family had its own concoction. We could smell the aromatic scents of the clove, cinnamon and roseleaf from blocks away.

IRAQI BAHARAT

YIELD: APPROXIMATELY 1 CUP (99 G)

3 tbsp (18 g) ground cinnamon

3 tbsp (18 g) ground allspice

3 tbsp (18 g) ground nutmeg

1 tsp ground ginger

2 tbsp (12 g) finely ground black pepper

1 tsp cardamom

¼ tsp ground cloves (optional)

1 tbsp (3 g) dried, ground roseleaf (optional)

In a medium bowl, mix all of the ingredients together and stir until fully combined. Transfer to an airtight spice container, and store in a cool, dark place or refrigerator until needed.

This recipe is for those who simply cannot get enough eggplant! Baharat eggplant is a great side dish and works perfectly with chicken, fish, lamb or meat or on its own alongside any grain. You can also use it as a base for a shakshuka (poached eggs in a sauce of tomatoes, roasted peppers and onions). Just break a few eggs once the stew is done and you'll have an eggplant-based shakshuka.

BAHARAT EGGPLANT AND CHICKPEA TOMATO STEW

YIELD: 4–5 SERVINGS

4 tbsp (60 ml) extra-virgin olive oil

1 onion, diced

4 cloves garlic, slivered

2 large eggplants, cut into medium cubes

½ cup (120 ml) water

1 cup (164 g) cooked chickpeas

4 tomatoes, diced

Salt and pepper, to taste

¼ tsp brown sugar

1 tsp Iraqi Baharat (page 41)

½ cup (60 g) chopped walnuts (optional)

½ bunch parsley, chopped

In a large saucepan, heat the olive oil over medium-low heat. Add the onion, and sauté for 10 to 12 minutes, or until golden brown. Add the garlic and sauté for 2 minutes. Add the eggplant and sauté for 10 minutes. Stir frequently.

Add the water, chickpeas, tomatoes, salt, pepper, brown sugar and Iraqi Baharat. Add the walnuts, if using. Stir well and let cook for 15 minutes, covered.

Remove from the heat and transfer to a serving bowl. Sprinkle with fresh parsley and serve.

Growing up, my family threw barbecues almost every holiday. I loved watching the women in my family making their kofta mixture by hand. Kofta is a Middle Eastern meatball or meatloaf of ground beef or lamb mixed with spices and onions. While my mom chopped the onions, my aunt finely diced the parsley. This recipe comes straight from my family's kitchen and makes for a great burger.

BAHARAT-SCENTED KOFTA

YIELD: 6 BURGERS

2 lb (900 g) ground beef

4 medium yellow onions, finely chopped

2 bunches parsley, stems removed and finely chopped

Salt and pepper, to taste

1 tbsp (5 g) Iraqi Baharat (page 41)

Preheat an outdoor grill to 300°F (150°C) or the oven to 350°F (175°C).

In a large bowl, add the ground beef, onions, parsley, salt, pepper and baharat. Mix well with your hands until fully incorporated. Let it rest for 15 minutes and then make burgers out of the mixture.

Cook the burgers on the grill for about 2 minutes on each side or in the oven for about 10 minutes total.

CHEF'S TIP: If you can find ground lamb fat, use it alongside leaner ground beef.

Mint and lamb go hand in hand, but when adding baharat to the mix, you're
creating a holy trinity of flavors. Baharat really complements and balances the lamb's
rich flavors. Topping the lamb with the mint pesto will finish this dish perfectly.

BAHARAT-SCENTED LAMB LOIN WITH MINT PESTO

YIELD: 4 SERVINGS

4 lamb loins or steaks (about 4 oz [113 g]) each

4 tbsp (60 ml) extra-virgin olive oil

Salt and pepper, to taste

2 tsp (4 g) Iraqi Baharat (page 41)

FOR THE MINT PESTO

¼ cup (30 g) walnuts

1 bunch fresh mint leaves, rinsed and dried

4 cloves garlic

1 tbsp (15 ml) lime juice

Zest of 1 lime or lemon

⅓ cup (80 ml) extra-virgin olive oil

Salt and pepper, to taste

Place the lamb on a tray or baking sheet, drizzle with the olive oil and rub the salt, pepper and Iraqi Baharat on both sides to coat the lamb. Cover the baking sheet with plastic wrap and set aside at room temperature for 1 hour so the meat will absorb all the flavors.

To make the mint pesto, place the walnuts, mint, garlic, lime juice and zest in a food processor. Pulse until everything is finely chopped and blended, but not too saucy. Pesto needs to have texture and crunchiness. Place the mixture in a medium bowl and add the olive oil. Stir well until fully incorporated. Season with salt and pepper.

In a large oiled cast-iron skillet over medium-high heat, add the lamb loin and sear on both sides for 3 to 5 minutes on each side, or until nicely browned. If you prefer your lamb medium rare, you're done. If you prefer your lamb medium to medium-well, place the skillet in a preheated oven at 375°F (190°C) for 10 minutes, or until cooked to your desired temperature.

Place the loins on plates and scoop 1 tablespoon (15 g) of mint pesto on each to serve.

CHEF'S TIP: For an added layer of flavor, spread 1 tablespoon (15 g) of raw tahini across each plate and place the loin over it. Garnish with a fresh mint sprig.

When I was a child, this sweet-and-sour meal was unique to Jews from Iraq.
Today, it's well-known throughout Israel.

BEET AND BAHARAT KIBBEH (RED KIBBEH)

YIELD: 8–10 SERVINGS

FOR THE SOUP

4 tbsp (60 ml) extra-virgin olive oil

1 large white onion, chopped

5 beets, cubed

½ celery rib, leaves, chopped

3 tbsp (45 g) tomato paste

1 tsp sugar, plus more to taste

Salt and pepper, to taste

Juice of ½ lemon

FOR THE KIBBEH DOUGH

1 cup (140 g) fine bulgur

2 cups (475 ml) warm water

1½ cups (240 g) semolina flour

1 tsp salt

2 tsp (10 ml) extra-virgin olive oil

FOR THE KIBBEH FILLING

2 tsp (10 ml) extra-virgin olive oil

1 white onion, finely chopped

1 lb (450 g) ground beef

2 tsp (4 g) Iraqi Baharat (page 41)

Salt and pepper, to taste

½ cup (60 g) pine nuts

¼ bunch parsley, finely chopped

To make the soup, heat the olive oil in a large soup pot. Add the onion, and sauté for 10 minutes, or until golden brown. Add the beets and celery. Sauté for 3 minutes. Add the tomato paste and stir until it dissolves. Add water so the pot is half full. Bring the soup to a boil and add the sugar, salt, pepper and lemon juice. Taste and adjust the seasoning. Let it simmer over low heat for about 30 minutes, or until the beets and celery are tender.

To make the kibbeh dough, in a large bowl, soak the bulgur in the water for 20 minutes, or until soft. Add the semolina flour, salt and oil, and mix into a soft, workable dough. Adjust the consistency with flour and water as needed.

To make the kibbeh filling, heat the olive oil in a large skillet, and sauté the onion for 10 minutes, or until golden. Add the ground beef and sauté for 10 minutes while adding the Iraqi Baharat, salt, pepper and pine nuts. Remove from the heat, add the parsley, adjust the seasoning and set aside.

You want the kibbeh dumpling to be thin. If the dough tears, you can easily patch it with a little extra dough. Grease your hands in oil and make small balls from the dough. Create a crater in the center of each ball. Add filling to the crater and slowly close up the balls. Gently drop each ball into the soup and let them simmer for about 20 minutes, or until fully cooked.

Ditch traditional meatloaf and explore the flavors baharat spice mix brings out in this all-American dish. You can still match it with your traditional fixings. In fact, it's quite wonderful with a sweet potato mash.

TURKEY MEATLOAF WITH RAISINS AND BAHARAT

YIELD: 8–10 SERVINGS

FOR THE MEATLOAF GLAZE

2 tbsp (30 g) tomato paste

Pinch of Iraqi Baharat (page 41)

1 tsp honey or silan (date syrup)

2 tbsp (30 ml) extra-virgin olive oil

FOR THE MEATLOAF

3 tbsp (45 ml) extra-virgin olive oil

½ onion, diced

2 celery ribs, diced

1 carrot, diced

2 lb (900 g) ground turkey

2 extra-large eggs, lightly beaten

¾ cup (45 g) chopped mushrooms

1 tsp Iraqi Baharat (page 41)

½ cup (20 g) chopped parsley

⅓ cup (16 g) minced scallions

2 cloves garlic, minced

1 tsp sweet paprika

1⅓ cups (140 g) panko or whole-grain breadcrumbs

1 cup (180 g) diced tomatoes

Salt and pepper, to taste

Preheat the oven to 375°F (190°C). Lightly oil a loaf pan.

To make the meatloaf glaze, in a medium bowl, add the tomato paste, baharat, honey and olive oil and whisk. Set aside.

To make the meatloaf, heat the olive oil in a saucepan over medium heat and when hot, add the onion, celery and carrot, and sauté for 10 minutes, or until the vegetables are tender and golden. Let the mixture cool for a few minutes.

In a large bowl, combine the saucepan contents, turkey, eggs, mushrooms, baharat, parsley, scallions, garlic, paprika, panko, tomatoes, salt and pepper. Knead by hand until the mixture is well combined.

Transfer the turkey mixture into the loaf pan. Pack it down gently. Brush the top of the meatloaf with the meatloaf glaze. Bake for 1 hour and allow it to sit for 10 minutes before serving.

CARAWAY

What would pastrami on rye be without caraway seeds? Dining at any Jewish delicatessen wouldn't be the same without caraway seeds—barrels of sour pickles included. A handful of these seeds give a slice of bread and a scoop of cabbage bites of punch that are just as earthy as they are sweet. When I say earthy, I mean tied to the earth.

A member of the carrot family, the caraway plant looks like a carrot with sprouts of thin, feathery green leaves protruding out from its 2-foot (61-cm) stem. Its roots can even be cooked down just like a carrot.

With warm, down-to-earth flavor agents, it's easy to see why mom-and-pop sandwich shops have been baking these tiny seeds into their loaves of bread for eons. In fact, rye bread was a staple during the Middle Ages and a main component of the common man's diet. But there's more to this fennel seed than meets the eye—and the tongue.

Caraway seeds alleviate heartburn, bloating, gas and stomach spasms. (Caraway oil works as well!) Some people even use caraway as a cough suppressant and to expel phlegm. It's even said to help women start menstruation, soothe menstrual cramps and increase the flow of breast milk. Who needs over-the-counter medications when you have caraway!?

This chapter, however, focuses on caraway seeds's other attribute: great taste. Whether making a salad or harissa paste (page 56), these little seeds will bring some pizzazz to your palate.

I love this combination! The caraway seeds ramp up the flavor and crunchiness that complements the Gorgonzola in a very special way.

FRISÉE, PEAR, GORGONZOLA AND CARAWAY SALAD

YIELD: 4 SERVINGS

2 tsp (4 g) whole caraway seeds

4 tbsp (60 ml) extra-virgin olive oil

2 tbsp (30 ml) red wine vinegar

1 tsp honey

1 tbsp (15 ml) Dijon mustard

Salt and pepper, to taste

5 cups (100 g) frisée

3 hard pears, sliced on a mandoline

½ cup (25 g) chopped fresh chives, divided

8 medium-thin slices Gorgonzola cheese

12 roasted hazelnuts, crushed

To toast the caraway seeds, heat a small skillet over medium heat and add the caraway seeds. Stir for 2 to 3 minutes, or until lightly toasted and their aroma is released. Remove from the heat and let the seeds cool.

In a medium bowl, add the oil, vinegar, honey, mustard, salt and pepper and whisk. Set aside.

In a large bowl, add the frisée, caraways seeds, pears and half the chives, and dress. Lightly mix the salad.

Divide the salad among four plates, and rest two slices of Gorgonzola on each salad. Sprinkle the crushed hazelnuts and remaining chives on top of each salad.

CHEF'S TIP: For added flavor, drizzle a little balsamic reduction over the salad.

Harissa is a mild pepper paste. The main ingredients are New Mexico chiles, a tabil mixture (see below), garlic as well as some olive oil for preservation. It is most closely associated with Tunisia, Libya and Algeria. In North Africa, cooks rely on harissa to add depth to cooked sauces, soups, meats and vegetables. When I was growing up we always had a container filled with this red goodness and we put it on everything: sandwiches, roasts, meatballs, sauces, pasta, potatoes . . . you name it! So here is a simple harissa recipe passed down from generation to generation.

HARISSA WITH CARAWAY, CUMIN AND CORIANDER

YIELD: APPROXIMATELY 2 CUPS (512 G)

12–14 dried New Mexico chiles

1 tbsp (5 g) tabil spice mix or
1 tsp each of cumin, caraway and coriander

4 tbsp (60 ml) extra-virgin olive oil, or more as needed

1½ tsp (8 g) Celtic salt

8–12 cloves garlic

Place the chile peppers in a medium bowl, cover with water and let sit for about 2 hours, or until the chiles soften. Drain the chile peppers. Remove the stems of each pepper, but keep the seeds and transfer them to the bowl of a food processor with the tabil, olive oil, salt and garlic. Purée, stopping occasionally to scrape down the sides of the bowl, until the paste is smooth but not completely puréed. It should be a bit crunchy.

Transfer to a 1-pint (475-ml) glass jar and top it with oil until the ingredients are submerged, leaving at least ½ inch (1.3 cm) of oil above the paste. Harissa paste will keep for up to 3 weeks in the refrigerator.

TABIL FOR YOUR TABLE: Tabil is an Algerian and Tunisian spice mixture generally consisting of ground coriander seeds, caraway seeds and cumin. Other variations may include the addition of garlic powder, chili powder, rose flower powder, dried ground mint or even a touch of clove. I used to use only cumin in my harissa, but a Tunisian friend suggested I try a classic tabil mix, and I'm hooked! Tabil is wonderful in many dishes and sauces, and you can make your own mix, store it in a cool place and use it whether you need to add a kick to your meatballs, chicken or seared tuna. Definitely use it in your harissa!

Served in the Near and Middle East, the Balkans and some parts of Central Asia, meze (or mezze) is a selection of small dishes served to start a meal or to accompany alcoholic drinks. A childhood favorite meze from my father's side of the family is carrots in caraway and harissa. The natural sweetness of the carrots and the rich spices work here to create something not found in other meze selections. This is served family style, so I plan on at least one carrot per person.

TUNISIAN CARAWAY CARROT SALAD

YIELD: 6 APPETIZER SERVINGS

6 medium-to-large carrots

4 qt (4 L) salted water

1 tsp ground caraway seeds

6 cloves garlic, slivered

Juice of 1 lemon

4 tbsp (60 ml) extra-virgin olive oil

Salt and pepper, to taste

1 tbsp (5 g) Harissa with Caraway, Cumin and Coriander (page 56) or red pepper flakes

Small bunch cilantro, chopped

In a medium pot, cook the carrots in the salted water over medium heat for 20 minutes, or until the carrots are tender but not too soft. Remove the carrots from the pot and slice them into ⅓-inch (8-mm)-thick slices.

In a large bowl, place the carrots, caraway, garlic, lemon juice, olive oil, salt, pepper and harissa. If you don't have harissa and would like to add some extra kick, use red pepper flakes instead. Mix well, adjust the seasoning, sprinkle the cilantro over the salad and serve.

CHEF'S TIP: Serve this alongside other appetizers, such as hummus, tahini, olives and pita bread.

CARDAMOM

Indian cuisine is a fantastic culinary world filled with curries, masala-spiced dishes and tandoori-cooked meats. After digging into a bowl of basmati rice, you may wonder what gave this Himalayan long-grain rice so much flavor. The answer is cardamom. Native to southern India, this plant can reach up to 30 feet (9 m) tall. Cardamom comes from the small, brown-black seeds that are found in the plant's black, white, red and green pods.

Cardamom's flavor is bold, smoky and distinct enough to make it the third-most expensive spice in the world. Depending on which cardamom spice you choose, it can even be fruity with hints of ginger. It has also been used throughout history to aid with digestion and appetite, relieve heartburn and irritable bowel syndrome and support the immune system. Cardamom is also used in soaps, creams and perfumes.

There are boundless variations of dishes that include cardamom. I personally enjoy putting it in my coffee, but it also goes well with meats, vegetables and especially pastries like my Cardamom Vanilla Apricot Pie (page 64).

You can get creative with cardamom, so feel free to experiment!

Cardamom is wonderfully aromatic and adds many deep and smoky tones to a roasted chicken dish. Most people can't pinpoint the cardamom in this dish as this spice is underutilized in Western kitchens. I think it's time to let it shine, and so will you after serving this tantalizing dish!

CARDAMOM-ROASTED CHICKEN

YIELD: 4 SERVINGS

1 cup (240 ml) extra-virgin olive oil

2 tsp (4 g) ground cardamom

1 tsp sweet paprika

2 tbsp (16 g) grated lemon zest

8 cloves garlic, slivered

1 tsp kosher salt, plus more to taste

¼ tsp freshly ground pepper, plus more to taste

1 whole chicken (2–3 lb [900–1350 g])

6 potatoes, cut into ¼" (6-mm)-thick rounds

2 lemons, cut into 1" (2.5-cm)-thick rounds

1 cup (180 g) pitted kalamata olives

A few thyme sprigs, for garnishing

Preheat the oven to 400°F (200°C).

In a small bowl, combine the olive oil, cardamom, paprika, lemon zest, garlic, salt and pepper. Set aside.

Place the chicken on a cutting board and slide your fingers between the flesh and the skin of the chicken to separate the skin from the flesh. Use a teaspoon and your fingers to inject the flavored oil into the space between the flesh and the skin, as well as all over the outside of the skin until the chicken is fully covered. Don't use all the oil as you will toss the potatoes in it as well. Set aside.

In a medium bowl, toss the potatoes in the remaining oil mixture. Add the lemons and the olives, season with salt and pepper and transfer to a roasting pan.

Place the chicken on top of the potatoes and cover with aluminum foil. Roast for about 90 minutes, or until the chicken is completely cooked through. Remove the foil and let the chicken roast for another 30 minutes, or until fully browned. Arrange the chicken over the potatoes in a serving platter. Garnish with the fresh thyme sprigs.

I'm going to let you in on a little secret. As much as I love cooking, I am not as fond of baking. But I do love baked goods, especially spiced ones. If you're like me, my advice is to always have ready-made, high-quality, store-bought filo dough, pie crusts and pizza dough in the freezer. So, whether or not you happen to have some pie crusts in the freezer, you're going to love the flavor combination of vanilla, apricot and cardamom.

CARDAMOM VANILLA APRICOT PIE

YIELD: 8 SERVINGS

20 apricots, pitted and halved

1 cup (225 g) packed brown sugar

¼ cup (35 g) all-purpose flour

1 tsp ground cardamom

1 tbsp (15 ml) vanilla extract

2 pie crusts, store-bought or homemade

2 tbsp (30 g) unsalted butter

1 egg yolk

1 tbsp (15 g) coarse sugar

Vanilla ice cream, for serving (optional)

Preheat the oven to 375°F (190°C).

In a large bowl, combine the apricots, brown sugar, flour, cardamom and vanilla. Carefully stir everything together and let it rest for about 30 minutes to marinate.

Roll out the pie crusts until the top dough disk is approximately 9 inches (23 cm) in diameter and the bottom dough disk is approximately 12 inches (30 cm) in diameter.

Place the bottom dough disk in the pan, letting its edges hang over the lip of the pie pan. Scoop the apricot mix to fill the pan and then top with little dollops of the butter in between the apricots. Place the top pie crust over the fruit mix and roll the edge of the pastries together. Trim away any excess dough if necessary.

Brush the pie crust with the egg yolk and sprinkle with the sugar. Before placing in the oven, be sure to make a few slits in the pie to let hot air escape. Bake for 20 to 30 minutes while watching the top crust, making sure to not over-brown it. Cover the pie with aluminum foil and bake for an additional 30 minutes, or until the dough has fully baked.

Top with vanilla ice cream, if desired, and serve.

This is a wonderful soup originating from the traditional Yemenite Jewish community. Like other dishes brought by the various Jewish communities to Israel as they migrated there, it became a staple of the new Israeli cuisine as it's been adopted by so many chefs and families for its special spiced aromas and comforting qualities. The cardamom here is part of a spice mix called hawaij, which you can find in specialty grocery stores. To make a vegetarian version, you can replace the meat with a mix of wild and dried mushrooms.

CARDAMOM YEMENITE BEEF SOUP

YIELD: 12–16 SERVINGS

½ cup (120 ml) extra-virgin olive oil, divided

2 lb (900 g) beef stew meat or 1 whole chicken, cut up

Salt and pepper, to taste

2 medium onions, diced

2–3 beef bones (optional)

6 qt (6 L) water

1 tbsp (5 g) hawaij spice blend

6 cloves garlic, minced

4 medium russet potatoes, peeled and cut into large cubes

2–3 celery ribs with leaves, cut into large segments

1 large bunch cilantro

In a large soup pot, heat ¼ cup (60 ml) of the olive oil over medium-high heat. Add the meat and brown it for about 15 minutes, turning often with a spatula. Move the meat to a bowl and season with salt and pepper.

Add the remaining ¼ cup (60 ml) olive oil to the pot and add the diced onions. Sauté for 10 to 12 minutes, or until translucent.

Add the meat back to the pot along with the bones (if using) and the water and bring to a simmer. Skim off any foam that rises to the top. Stir in the hawaij mix, salt, pepper and the garlic. Reduce the heat to low and simmer for 2 hours.

Once the meat starts getting soft and tender, add the potatoes and celery and cook for 1 hour. If using mushrooms, add them to the soup at the same time as the potatoes and celery. Add the cilantro 15 minutes before the soup is done. Adjust the seasonings and serve.

CHEF'S TIP: Serve this soup with fresh pita, Cumin Cardamom Yemenite S'chug (page 114) and a fresh Israeli salad.

I'm not sure how I figured out that cardamom goes so well with sweet potatoes, but once I did, I never baked sweet potatoes without it again. Then I added cardamom to carrots, pumpkins and butternut squash and those tasted excellent as well. So, why not throw all these healthy veggies together for an orange celebration?! Mix and match the veggies based on taste and availability and play around with the size and shape of the veggies. You really can't go wrong with this perfect Thanksgiving dish.

MAPLE AND CARDAMOM-ROASTED ORANGE VEGETABLES

YIELD: 8 SERVINGS

3 sweet potatoes, peeled and cut into 1½" (3.8-cm) cubes or slices

1 butternut squash, peeled and cut into 1½" (3.8-cm) cubes or slices

4 carrots, peeled and cut into 1½" (3.8-cm)-thick rounds

½ lb (230 g) pumpkin, cut into 1½" (3.8-cm) cubes or slices

1 cup (240 ml) extra-virgin olive oil

Salt and pepper, to taste

2 tbsp (12 g) ground cardamom

½ cup (120 ml) maple syrup

2–3 thyme sprigs

Preheat the oven to 400°F (200°C).

In a large bowl, add the sweet potatoes, butternut squash, carrots and pumpkin. Drizzle with the olive oil. Add the salt, pepper, cardamom and maple syrup. Massage the mixture until the vegetables are equally covered.

Transfer the vegetables into a large roasting pan. Add the thyme and roast for 1 hour, or until tender. Flip the vegetables about halfway through the roasting process.

CINNAMON

Cinnamon always melts my heart and palate. Its aroma is an intoxicating gift from Mother Earth delivered by trees. Obtained from the inner bark of several tree species from the genus *Cinnamomum*, cinnamon is used in the Middle East for both sweet and savory dishes. With varying types yielding different flavor profiles and packaged in ground and stick form, there's a lot to choose from. But no matter the texture and where it's from, cinnamon's intensely warm flavors will enhance any dish you craft, whether it's a batch of cookies or Cinnamon-Scented Moroccan Couscous (page 74). You probably already have cinnamon on hand, but these recipes will show you new and exciting ways to incorporate this popular spice into your meals.

Prized for its medicinal properties, doctors have been prescribing cinnamon as a natural aid to cure the common cold since the Middle Ages, and today scientists are conducting clinical trials to put this age-old theory to the test. One neuroscientist recently evaluated cinnamon's benefits on those suffering from multiple sclerosis (MS) and found that symptoms could be alleviated by using this natural anti-inflammatory spice. However, there is much more research to be done as scientists also look into cinnamon's effects on reducing glucose levels, improving blood pressure and more.

When I have zero time and still want to make an alluring dessert, I use an old trick. I bake cored apples sprinkled with brown sugar and cinnamon and then stuff them with vanilla ice cream mixed with broken pieces of baklava. I drizzle some honey or silan on top and serve. Easy, breezy, gorgeous!

CINNAMON BAKED APPLES WITH BAKLAVA ICE CREAM

YIELD: 4 SERVINGS

2 tsp (10 g) brown sugar

1 tsp ground cinnamon

4 large Gala apples

4 large scoops vanilla ice cream

4 pieces pistachio baklava, chopped

Honey or silan (date syrup), to taste

Roasted pistachios, for garnishing (optional)

Preheat the oven to 375°F (190°C). Lightly oil a baking sheet. Remove the ice cream from the freezer so it will be slightly soft when needed.

In a small bowl, mix together the brown sugar and cinnamon. Set aside.

Wash the apples and using an apple corer, core out the center of the apples. Use a paring knife to make a little more space within the center of the apples.

Place the apples on the baking sheet. If the apples can't stand on their own, cut the bottoms so they are flat. Sprinkle the sugar and cinnamon mix inside and all around each apple. Bake for 15 to 20 minutes, or until the apples are soft and tender but still holding their shape.

While the apples are cooking, fold the ice cream and chopped baklava in a bowl and place in the freezer. When ready to serve, place the warm apples on a serving plate and scoop the ice cream on top of the apples. Some of the ice cream will melt into the core. Drizzle with honey or silan and sprinkle a few roasted pistachios on the plate, if desired.

CHEF'S TIP: If you don't have baklava handy, you can use cookies or biscotti crumbled into your ice cream. Another way to enhance the flavor is to drizzle a few teaspoons of orange blossom water over it.

My aunt married a Moroccan Jew when I was a little boy. Her husband opened my palate to new versions of dishes I already knew. For instance, when I first tasted his sweet Moroccan couscous, I was in awe because I was so used to our savory and stew-like Tunisian version. So once I had his, I couldn't decide which I liked best. Thankfully, I don't have to choose; I can simply enjoy both!

CINNAMON-SCENTED MOROCCAN COUSCOUS WITH DRIED FRUIT

YIELD: 10 SERVINGS

2 tbsp (30 ml) extra-virgin olive oil

½ cup (70 g) chopped cipollini onions

12 dried apricots

12 pitted prunes

1 cup (140 g) raisins

1 tsp ground cinnamon

4 cinnamon sticks

½ tsp brown sugar (optional)

Salt and pepper, to taste

4 cups (1 L) vegetable stock or water, divided

1 cup (164 g) cooked chickpeas, drained

1 lb (450 g) dried couscous

Small bunch chives, chopped

½ cup (50 g) sliced roasted or raw almonds

Preheat the oven to 400°F (200°C).

In a large skillet, heat the oil over medium-high heat. Once the oil is hot, add the onions and sauté for 10 minutes, or until golden. Add the apricots, prunes, raisins, ground cinnamon, cinnamon sticks, brown sugar (if using), salt and pepper. Sauté over low heat for 10 minutes. Add ½ cup (120 ml) of the vegetable stock and the chickpeas. Stir well and cook for 10 minutes. Set aside.

In a soup pot, bring the remaining 3½ cups (820 ml) of vegetable stock to a boil over high heat. Place the couscous in an ovenproof dish. Mix in the dried fruit mix. Pour the boiling vegetable stock over the couscous and cover tightly with aluminum foil.

Turn off the oven and place the couscous in the oven for 15 minutes, or until all the liquids have been absorbed.

Fluff the couscous and transfer to a serving dish. Sprinkle with the chives and almonds.

I love the cone-shaped earthenware pots that give tagine dishes their name. The cone-like shape allows heat to build up at the top of the cone, which works to build up moisture. The moisture drips back down into the ingredients, allowing for a very moist, aromatic and tender dish. This recipe fuses dried fruit, cinnamon and lamb: an irresistible celebration of flavors and aromas.

LAMB TAGINE WITH CINNAMON APRICOTS AND PRUNES

YIELD: 3-4 SERVINGS

2 tbsp (30 ml) extra-virgin olive oil

1 lb (450 g) lamb meat, cubed

2 onions, sliced

2 carrots, sliced

1 tsp ground cumin

2 cloves garlic, minced

½ tsp finely grated ginger

1 tsp paprika

4 cups (1 L) water

Pinch of saffron threads

1 tsp ground cinnamon

4 cinnamon sticks

Salt and pepper, to taste

½ cup (90 g) pitted prunes

½ cup (90 g) dried apricots

Preheat the oven to 350°F (175°C).

In a heavy pot, heat the oil over medium heat. Brown the lamb in two batches, 4 to 5 minutes each, turning occasionally. Remove and set aside. Reduce the heat to low.

Add the onions to the pot and cook for 10 minutes, or until golden. Stir in the carrots, cumin, garlic, ginger and paprika. Cook for 1 minute, stirring frequently. Pour in the water and add the saffron, ground cinnamon, cinnamon sticks, salt and pepper. Check for flavor, bring to a simmer and return the lamb to the pot. Cover tightly, transfer to the oven and bake for 1 hour.

Stir in the prunes and apricots and make sure all of the lamb pieces are fully covered in liquid. Cover and bake for another 30 to 45 minutes, or until the lamb is very tender.

CHEF'S TIP: You can transfer the meal to a traditional tagine after returning the lamb to the pot. Serving in a tagine creates a more authentic and dramatic presentation. Feel free to transfer to a tagine after preparing the meal, and serve with or over couscous or basmati rice.

Couscous is traditionally steamed in a couscoussier, which is a two-part pot. The bottom is a tall soup pot and the second is the steamer that sits right on top where the couscous gets steamed and cooked. Making traditional couscous takes time and patience, but the result is superior to the instant couscous you'll find in the grocery store. Traditional couscous is fluffy (never sticky!), moist and very airy, and you can taste each grain as it hits your palate.

In addition to your couscoussier, you'll need a traditional couscous sifter (which is a large, round metal sifter) to eliminate any clumps of grain that normally occur, and a large bowl to mix the couscous with oil and water between steaming sessions.

HOW TO STEAM COUSCOUS THE TRADITIONAL TUNISIAN MOROCCAN WAY

YIELD: 10 SERVINGS

5 qt (4.7 L) water for steaming, plus 6 cups (1.4 L), divided

2 lb (900 g) couscous

4 tbsp (60 ml) canola or sunflower oil, plus more as needed

2 tsp (10 g) salt

Oil the steamer part of your couscoussier. Bring 5 quarts (4.7 L) of water to a boil in the bottom part of the couscoussier. While the water heats up, prepare the grain for steaming.

In a large bowl, combine the couscous, oil and 1 cup (240 ml) of the water, and mix well for about 3 minutes with your hands. Distribute the liquids as equally as possible and let the grains absorb them. Try to get rid of any clumps. Transfer the couscous to the oiled steamer. Pack it so the steam goes through the couscous easily and cooks the grain. Place the steamer atop the pot. Steam the couscous for 30 minutes.

Remove the steamed couscous from the steamer and place back into the bowl. Add 2 cups (475 ml) of the water and the salt and mix very well. At this point you can use a fork to "open" the couscous as we say, which really means to get the grain airy and fluffy.

Once the liquid is absorbed, use the couscous sifter and force the couscous through it, batch by batch. This action helps get rid of all the clumps, which tend to occur.

Place the couscous into the steamer for 20 minutes. Remove the couscous from the steamer and place back into the bowl. Add the remaining 3 cups (700 ml) of water and work the grain with your hands or fork for about 3 minutes. Let the grains absorb the water. Working batch by batch, force the couscous through the sifter until all the clumps are gone and the remaining couscous is light and airy. Now you can return the couscous to the steamer and steam for the final time for about 20 minutes.

Every Friday in the early afternoon before Shabbat arrived, my father and I would visit my grandmother, and she would serve us a traditional Tunisian lunch that consisted of couscous with soup and mahshi. I looked forward to those lunches as her mahshi meatballs were so juicy and flavorful. I miss my grandmother, I miss those Friday afternoons and every time I make these, I send a blessing to her soul.

MAHSHI CINNAMON-SCENTED TUNISIAN MEATBALLS

YIELD: APPROXIMATELY 20 MEATBALLS

1 lb (450 g) ground turkey or beef

1 large onion, finely chopped

1 bunch cilantro, chopped (leaves only)

½ bunch parsley, chopped (leaves only)

4 eggs, divided

1 tsp ground cinnamon

½ tsp turmeric

1 tsp salt

Freshly ground black pepper, to taste

2 large slices day-old challah or crusty bread, soaked in water for 10 minutes

1 tsp Harissa with Caraway, Cumin and Coriander (page 56) or tomato paste

1 cup (240 ml) extra-virgin olive oil, or more as needed

1 cup (125 g) all-purpose flour

Place the ground turkey in a large bowl and add the onion. Squeeze the cilantro and parsley leaves to remove some of the liquid, and add to the bowl. Add 2 eggs, the cinnamon, turmeric, salt and pepper. Squeeze the excess water out of the bread and add to the mix. Work the mixture with your hands until thoroughly combined and set aside.

In a small bowl, whisk together the remaining 2 eggs and the harissa and set aside.

In a skillet, heat the oil over medium-high heat. If the oil doesn't reach half the height of the meatballs, add more.

Create flat, oval-shaped meatballs with the turkey mixture. Place the flour on a plate or in a shallow bowl. Dip each meatball first in the flour, covering them fully. Then dip each into the egg and harissa mix and fry over medium-low heat for about 15 minutes, flipping halfway through.

Before serving, place the cooked meatballs on paper towels to absorb any excess oil.

CHEF'S TIP: These meatballs are traditionally served alongside couscous, and some like to squeeze fresh lemon juice on top.

CLOVE

A friend once asked me, "If you could travel to any time or place in the world, where would you go?" After half of a split second, there was only one place I would rather be than my adopted home in Miami Beach: the Spice Islands in the 1700s. I am The Spice Detective after all, right?

The Maluku Islands are nestled just on the equator, north of Australia and west of New Guinea. And located on a small island in Eastern Indonesia, not too far from the white sand beaches and serene ocean waters, there's a 400-year-old clove tree named Afo. And at one point, this tree produced something more precious than gold: cloves. And thanks to a Frenchman, named Pierre Poivre, this tree ended the Dutch monopoly on cloves. As the story goes, in 1750, Poivre snuck onto the island and stole some of Afo's precious seedlings and brought them to Mauritius and then to Zanzibar, a small region in Tanzania. I would have loved to have been there to watch Poivre change spice history with his daring escapade.

Stories, just like recipes, are passed on, rewritten and adjusted. Yet there is one fact that remains as told: the clove was once worth more than gold. So to pay homage to a luxury, an indulgence, an extravagance, I am dedicating this chapter to clove.

Whisk it in your ice cream, bake it in butter cookies and mix it in my "cheesecake" mousse (page 89). It will bring opulence to your evening dinner party and fortune to your taste buds!

What about traditional medicine, you ask? That's easy! Clove oil is used for bad breath, intestinal gas, nausea and vomiting. My grandmother used to apply clove directly to the gums for toothaches. In addition, not only is clove oil known for its antifungal and antiseptic treatments, it was used in ancient times as an aphrodisiac and stimulant agent. That's more than enough to get you excited about clove.

You won't know how delicious and exotic beets with clove taste until you try it. A little clove goes a long way and brings sweet aromas and earthy tones to this beloved root vegetable. These beets can be served as a side dish over tahini or mint yogurt sauce or incorporated into your favorite salads.

CLOVE-ROASTED RED AND GOLDEN BEETS

YIELD: 4-6 SERVINGS

8 golden and red beets, washed, peeled and quartered

4 tbsp (60 ml) extra-virgin olive oil

1 tsp whole cloves

5 cloves garlic, slivered

Salt and pepper, to taste

4 tbsp (60 ml) balsamic vinegar reduction (can be reduced at home or bought in the gourmet section of many grocery stores)

A few chive sprigs, chopped

Preheat the oven to 425°F (220°C).

In a bowl, toss the beets with the oil, cloves, garlic, salt and pepper. Mix to coat the beets.

Place the beets on a baking sheet or roasting pan and cover with aluminum foil. Roast for approximately 20 to 30 minutes, or until the beets are tender.

Remove from the pan and place on a serving platter. Drizzle with the balsamic reduction and chopped chives.

CHEF'S TIP: For a variation, make mint yogurt sauce to serve with the beets. Chop small bunches of mint leaves and mix into 1 cup (240 g) plain, full-fat yogurt. Mix well and add 1 teaspoon of lime zest as well as salt and pepper, to taste.

Clove is impossibly fragrant. Match with honey and orange for a superb, balanced flavor. When the clove is whole it is less intense than when in powder form, so roasting it whole with the chicken will release the aroma but won't overpower the meat.

CORNISH HEN ROASTED WITH CLOVE, HONEY AND ORANGE

YIELD: 4 SERVINGS

1 cup (240 ml) extra-virgin olive oil, divided

2 tbsp (40 g) honey

4 Cornish hens, 1½–2 lb (680–900 g) each

Salt and pepper, to taste

2 oranges, quartered

A handful of whole cloves

12 cloves garlic, slivered

4 thyme sprigs

1 cup (240 ml) white wine

2–4 carrots, cut into bâtonnets (sticks) (optional)

Preheat the oven to 400°F (200°C). Grease a large roasting pan with ½ cup (120 ml) of the olive oil.

In a medium bowl, whisk the honey with the remaining ½ cup (120 ml) olive oil.

Rub the hens with the mixture. Insert some of the mixture into the cavity and under the skin as well. Season the hens with salt and pepper. Place a quarter of an orange, a few cloves and a few slivers of garlic in the cavity of each hen.

Arrange the hens on the roasting pan. Place the remaining garlic, cloves and thyme sprigs around the hens and pour the white wine into the roasting pan. Add the carrots, if using. Cover in aluminum foil and roast for 40 minutes.

Reduce the oven temperature to 350°F (175°C). Uncover the hens and continue roasting until the hens are browned.

CHEF'S TIP: To make a sauce, place the remaining liquids from the roasting pan along with the garlic and cloves into a small saucepan. Simmer until the sauce is reduced. Fix the seasoning as necessary and pour over the hens.

This is a no-bake, easy-to-make "cheesecake" mousse. I serve it as a sweet bite crowd-pleaser at some of our events. The sweet, clove-spiced mousse works perfectly inside a fresh strawberry "cup" and it looks so pretty.

FRESH STRAWBERRIES STUFFED WITH CLOVE-SPICED "CHEESECAKE" MOUSSE

YIELD: 40 STRAWBERRIES

40 strawberries, washed and dried

1 lb (450 g) mascarpone cheese

4 oz (113 g) cream cheese

1 tsp vanilla extract

¼ tsp ground cloves

1–2 tbsp (15–30 ml) orange-flavored liqueur, such as Grand Marnier

2 tbsp (16 g) powdered sugar (or to taste)

Zest of 3 limes, for garnishing

To prepare the strawberry "cups," cut off the tops of the strawberries and cut a thin slice off the bottoms so that they can stand up. With a small melon baller, core the center of the strawberries.

If you don't have a melon baller, use a paring knife, and while using your thumb to guide the knife, gently cut the inside and scoop out the center to create space for the mousse.

To prepare the mousse, place the mascarpone, cream cheese, vanilla extract, cloves, orange-flavored liqueur and powdered sugar in a bowl. With a hand mixer, whip until smooth. Taste and adjust the sugar to your liking.

Transfer the mousse into a pastry bag with a star tip. If you don't have a pastry bag, cut a small piece of one corner of a resealable bag. Working one strawberry at a time, fill the "cup" with the mousse, creating a small mound about ½ inch (1.3 cm) high. Sprinkle a pinch of lime zest atop the mousse and serve.

My take on Jamaican jerk chicken is a fun recipe for your barbecue days, and it doesn't need a long time to marinate. This will add a kick to your traditional chicken wing recipe with no additional sauce needed.

GRILLED MIDDLE EASTERN JERK CHICKEN WINGS

YIELD: 12 WINGS

4 cloves garlic, minced

½ tsp ground cloves

1 tsp hot paprika, cayenne or chili powder

2 tsp (10 g) brown sugar

¼ tsp ground cinnamon

1 tbsp (2 g) dried mint leaves

½ tsp ground allspice

½ tsp cumin

Salt and pepper, to taste

3 tbsp (45 ml) extra-virgin olive oil

12 chicken wings, approximately 2 lb (900 g) total, skin on

Fresh salad, for serving (optional)

Lime wedges, for serving (optional)

Preheat an outdoor grill to medium-low or the oven to 400°F (200°C).

In a large bowl, mix together the garlic, cloves, hot paprika, brown sugar, cinnamon, mint, allspice, cumin, salt and pepper. Add the olive oil and mix until a thick paste forms. If necessary, add more oil.

Place the wings in the bowl and massage well to cover on all sides. Let them rest for 15 to 25 minutes.

Grill the wings for approximately 10 minutes on each side, or bake them in the oven for 30 to 40 minutes, or until cooked through with crispy, charred skin. Serve with a fresh salad and lime wedges, if desired.

CORIANDER

Yes, I call myself The Spice Detective, and like Sherlock Holmes, I like to think I'm the master of investigation for very powerful clients. Today, in this episode, coriander has asked for my help because it's suffering from an identity crisis. Is it coriander or is it cilantro? Let's look at the evidence:

Both originate from the same species, *Coriandrum sativum*, a member of the Apiaceae family. Widely used as a medicinal plant, *C. sativum* possesses biological properties that have been used to treat skin inflammation, anemia, high cholesterol levels and indigestion. Coriander seeds are rich in copper, magnesium, iron, potassium, manganese and zinc. These vital minerals help improve metabolism, increase red-blood cell count and regulate blood pressure.

Depending on the region, coriander and cilantro have different names. In North America, we refer to the leaves and stalks of this plant as cilantro. Its dried fruits, we call coriander seeds. Outside of North America, the leaves and stalks of *C. sativum* are referred to as coriander, and its dried fruits are known as coriander seeds.

So, based on all of the evidence, coriander is a spice. However, if I were at home in the Holy Land, we would have to reopen this case for further investigation. Now, back to the tasting table!

When crushed, these little fruit seeds extract a lemony, citrus flavor that emerges when cooked. Its subtle flavors are like seeing a ghost. You know it's there, but you just can't put your finger on it. Try adding it to banana cookies (page 100), potato soup or my green shakshuka (page 99). Its earthy textures are engaging, and when smelled, inviting. And for a coriander tea, boil a teaspoon of seeds and then add a little honey. It's quite soothing and may help ease constipation.

When you think about stir-fry, you immediately conjure up Asian kitchens, but there are other flavors of stir-fry to try. This recipe is light and healthy and explores the taste of chicken seasoned with coriander and maple.

CORIANDER CHICKEN AND BRUSSELS SPROUT STIR-FRY

YIELD: 4–6 SERVINGS

4 tbsp (60 ml) extra-virgin olive oil, divided

8 boneless, skinless chicken thighs (3–5 oz [84–140 g] each), cut into ¾" (2-cm) strips

4 cloves garlic, slivered

Salt and pepper, to taste

2 tsp (4 g) ground coriander

1 shallot, chopped

1 lb (450 g) Brussels sprouts, trimmed and halved

Slivered almonds (optional)

Walnuts (optional)

1–2 tbsp (15–30 ml) maple syrup

½ cup (25 g) chopped scallions, divided

In a large wok, heat 2 tablespoons (30 ml) of olive oil over medium-high heat. Add the chicken strips and garlic and stir-fry for a few minutes. Season with the salt, pepper and coriander and mix well. Keep stirring until the chicken is no longer pink. Remove from the wok and set aside.

Using the same wok, pour in the remaining 2 tablespoons (30 ml) of oil and add the shallot. Sauté for 2 minutes and add the Brussels sprouts, stirring occasionally for 10 minutes, or until the Brussels sprouts start to soften.

Return the chicken to the wok. Stir and add the nuts (if using), maple syrup and ¼ cup (12 g) of the scallions. Taste and adjust the seasonings, if necessary.

Continue to stir-fry until the chicken is fully cooked and the Brussels sprouts are soft but not mushy. Transfer to a serving platter and sprinkle with the remaining ¼ cup (12 g) scallions.

CHEF'S TIP: This tastes great served with jasmine rice.

When you are out of dinner ideas and need a quick, healthy-yet-fragrant fish dish,
look no further than this fillet of wild salmon paired with toasted coriander.
Easy, breezy and delicious.

CORIANDER-CRUSTED SALMON FILLET

YIELD: 6 SERVINGS

4 tbsp (24 g) whole coriander seeds

2 tbsp (12 g) sesame seeds

1 tsp sumac

Salt and pepper, to taste

Zest of 1 lime

6 salmon fillets (5–6 oz [140–168 g] each), skin on

9 tbsp (135 ml) extra-virgin olive oil, divided

Vegetables, potatoes, fresh greens or dill yogurt, for serving (optional)

In a medium skillet, toast the coriander seeds over medium-high heat for 3 to 5 minutes, or until fragrant and a little darker. Stir often with a wooden spoon. With either a pestle and mortar or grinder, grind the toasted coriander seeds to a medium consistency.

In a medium bowl, place the coriander, sesame seeds, sumac, salt, pepper and lime zest and mix well.

Rub both sides of each salmon fillet with 1 tablespoon (15 ml) of the olive oil but only press the flesh side of the fillets in the coriander mix to coat. Leave the fish to rest for 30 minutes.

Warm 3 tablespoons (45 ml) of oil in a large, ovenproof, nonstick skillet over medium-high heat until the oil is hot. Place the fillets in the skillet skin side down. Sear until the skin is browned and crispy, about 10 minutes. Turn and cook until the fish has reached the desired temperature, or 2 to 3 minutes for medium-rare. Repeat for the remaining fillets.

Serve over vegetables, potatoes or fresh greens with a side of dill yogurt, if desired.

No matter how much you love classic tomato shakshuka, eventually you'll need to have something else for breakfast, and for that reason, chefs in Israel came up with this delicious alternative known as the green shakshuka. Made with spinach, leek and chard melting into a creamy sauce scented with coriander and topped with eggs, this is my kind of sinful breakfast!

CORIANDER GREEN SHAKSHUKA

YIELD: 4 SERVINGS

4 qt (4 L) water

1 tbsp (15 g) salt, plus more to taste

2 bunches Swiss chard

3 tbsp (45 ml) extra-virgin olive oil

2 leeks, washed and sliced (green and white parts)

3 cloves garlic, slivered

1 jalapeño pepper, seeded and sliced (optional)

8 oz (230 g) spinach

½ cup (120 ml) heavy cream

Pepper, to taste

½ tsp ground coriander

½ tsp nutmeg

8 large eggs

⅓ cup (40 g) cubed feta cheese (optional)

Cilantro leaves, for garnishing

Pita bread, for serving (optional)

Israeli salad, for serving (optional)

Bring the water to a boil and add the salt. Separate the leaves and the stem of the chard. Chop the white stem and blanch the leaves for 2 minutes.

Heat the oil in a large skillet over medium-low heat. Sauté the leeks for about 10 minutes, or until softened. Add the garlic and jalapeño (if using) and cook for 2 minutes. Add the chard and spinach and cook over low heat while stirring for about 10 minutes, or until the leaves have softened. Add the cream, salt, pepper, coriander and nutmeg. Stir well. Cook for 5 minutes while bringing to a soft boil.

If you like your shakshuka saucy, add the eggs now. If you'd rather have it thicker, cook for an additional 5 to 10 minutes, until further reduced, and then gently add the eggs to the sauce. Cover and cook for 15 minutes over low heat.

Turn off the stove and add the feta cheese (if using). Cover and let stand for 5 minutes. Garnish with the cilantro and serve with plenty of pita and a fresh Israeli salad, if desired.

CHEF'S TIP: If you're an artichoke lover, feel free to add a few sliced artichoke hearts into the mix. Sauté it in when you add the chard. Yum!

I just can't get enough of how spices surprise and delight in the most unique ways. For instance, I bet most of you have never thought to pair banana and coriander before. Why would you, right?! Well, let me just say that the next time you find yourself with overripe bananas, make these cookies instead of banana bread. These spiced cookies are soft and delicious, almost like a coffee cake. I love adding pistachios to them, but feel free to add your favorite nuts.

SPICED CORIANDER BANANA COOKIES

YIELD: APPROXIMATELY 30 COOKIES

4 medium-ripe bananas, mashed

1 tsp baking soda

½ cup (113 g) unsalted butter, at room temperature

1 cup (225 g) packed brown sugar

1 egg

1 cup (140 g) shelled pistachios, walnuts or hazelnuts

2 cups (250 g) all-purpose flour

½ tsp ground coriander

½ tsp ground cinnamon

½ tsp ground nutmeg

Salt, to taste

Preheat the oven to 350°F (175°C). Line a baking sheet with parchment paper.

In a large bowl, mix the bananas and baking soda. Let this sit for a few minutes.

In a separate bowl, beat the butter and sugar together until light and fluffy. Add the egg and continue to beat until the mixture is light.

Mix the banana mixture into the butter mixture, add the pistachios and keep mixing. Add the flour, coriander, cinnamon, nutmeg and salt and mix well until fully blended and smooth.

Drop dollops of the mixture on the baking sheet, leaving 1½ inches (3.8 cm) of room between each dollop.

Bake for 10 to 15 minutes, or until golden brown. Let them cool on a cookie rack before serving. Store any uneaten cookies in the refrigerator.

CUMIN

You've heard that the sense of smell triggers memories. Every time I pull out a bottle of cumin, I'm reminded of wandering through the magical spice shops of my small hometown with my mom. The pungent, peppery scent always found a way to stand out and greet me as I entered the spice shop. Since I spent much of my youth learning the crafts of the kitchen from my mom, I picked up on the spices she used to make homestyle comfort dishes. From lamb skewers (page 106) and roasted beet salads (page 110) to breakfast shakshuka (page 113) and falafel (page 109), all I can say is that cumin is home. And I'm not the only child of a Jewish mother to have a beloved affection for cumin. Ancient Israelites have been cooking with cumin since the beginning of time. Some even call it the spice of the Bible.

Some of the benefits of adding cumin to your diet (besides taste!) include better digestion, a stronger liver, an improved immune system and more.

Cumin is a wonderful spice enhancement for fish, especially white fish. A little bit of this fragrant spice goes a long way! In this simple recipe, you will encrust the fish with cumin, sesame and paprika for a crispy crunch served with a touch of lemon.

CUMIN-CRUSTED CRISPY FISH FILLET

YIELD: 2 SERVINGS

2 tbsp (16 g) all-purpose flour

1 tsp ground cumin

1 tsp paprika

1 tbsp (6 g) white sesame seeds

Lemon salt or regular salt, to taste

Freshly ground pepper, to taste

1 egg white

2 white fish fillets, such as red snapper, sea bass or branzino (5–6 oz [140–168 g] each), skin on

4 tbsp (60 ml) canola oil

Green salad, for serving

Lemon wedges, for serving

In a shallow bowl or a pan, combine the flour, cumin, paprika, sesame seeds, salt and pepper.

In a separate bowl, beat the egg white.

Dip the fish in the egg white and then into the flour mixture, coating well and shaking off the excess.

In a skillet, heat the oil over medium-high heat. Once the oil is hot, fry the fillets for 5 minutes with the skin side down. Flip and fry for 3 minutes, or until cooked through.

Serve with a green salad and lemon wedges.

North African cuisine utilizes dried fruits in both savory and sweet dishes. I love to pair the gamy, earthy flavor of lamb with sweet dried fruit. In this recipe, the aromatic cumin and the sweetness of the prunes enhance and complement the lamb. Serve over rice and alongside a salad and you'll have a quick, delicious meal.

CUMIN LAMB AND PRUNE SKEWERS

YIELD: 8–10 SKEWERS

8–10 bamboo skewers

1 tbsp (6 g) ground cumin

1 tbsp (6 g) sweet paprika

¼ tsp ground cinnamon

Salt and pepper, to taste

1 lb (450 g) boneless lamb shoulder, cut into 1" (2.5-cm) cubes

4 tbsp (60 ml) extra-virgin olive oil

½ cup (90 g) pitted prunes

Rice, for serving

Israeli salad, for serving

Prepare the bamboo skewers by soaking them in water for 30 minutes. Preheat an outdoor grill to medium or heat a large, oiled skillet over medium heat.

In a small bowl, mix the cumin, paprika, cinnamon, salt and pepper.

Brush the lamb cubes with olive oil and dust the spice mix on them. Thread the spiced lamb and prunes onto the bamboo skewers, alternating between the two as you go.

Grill the skewers for 2 to 3 minutes on each side for medium, or 3 to 4 minutes for medium-well. Serve over rice with a side of Israeli salad.

CHEF'S TIP: You can substitute smoked or spicy paprika for the sweet paprika if you're looking for a slightly different taste.

What hasn't been said, written or sung about falafel? Thanks to the thousands of falafel shops in Israel, Tel Aviv is now recognized as the world capital of veganism. And indeed, falafel, with the assorted toppings, salads, pickles, hummus, tahini and spices, is a wholesome meal in a pita for vegans and non-vegans alike. Falafel was my childhood fast food, but remember, good falafel is not fast food: it takes love, time and patience. Soaking the chickpeas overnight is where we start.

CUMIN-SCENTED FALAFEL

YIELD: 36 BALLS

1 lb (450 g) dried chickpeas, soaked in water for 12 hours in the refrigerator

1 onion, finely chopped

3–5 cloves garlic

1 green mild pepper

1½ tsp (7 g) baking soda

½ cup (20 g) chopped fresh parsley

½ cup (10 g) chopped cilantro

1¾ tsp (5 g) salt

2 tsp (4 g) cumin

1 tbsp (6 g) sesame seeds

2 tsp (4 g) ground coriander

¼ tsp black pepper

Pinch of ground cardamom

Vegetable oil, for frying

Pita bread, for serving

Tahini, for serving

Fresh herbs, for serving

Place the chickpeas, onion, garlic, green pepper, baking soda, parsley and cilantro in a food processor. Process until fine but not smooth.

Place the chickpea mixture in a bowl and add the salt, cumin, sesame seeds, coriander, black pepper and cardamom. Mix well. Taste and adjust seasoning.

In a heavy skillet or fryer, heat the frying oil of your choice over medium heat. The oil should be warm but not burned.

With your hands, roll a ball of falafel mixture and drop it into the oil. Fry each ball for 3 to 5 minutes, or until browned and crispy. Serve the falafel warm in a pita sandwich with all the fixings or over tahini, sprinkled with some fresh herbs.

Like many of the recipes in this book, I grew up with this salad, eating it pretty much at least once a week. This dish comes from my father's side of the family, which is North African, and has become a staple in Israeli restaurants over the last 70 years. Many in the West don't realize how beautifully cumin complements the sweet, earthy flavor of beets, but trust me, this is a winner and is just so healthy.

CUMIN-DUSTED ROASTED BEET SALAD

YIELD: 8 SERVINGS

½ cup (120 ml) extra-virgin olive oil, plus more as needed

8 medium red beets

¼ tsp salt

Freshly ground black pepper, to taste

½ tsp ground cumin

Juice of 1 lemon

4 cloves garlic, sliced or slivered

3 tbsp (15 g) finely chopped fresh parsley, plus more for garnishing

Preheat the oven to 375°F (190°C) and grease a baking sheet with a little bit of olive oil.

Clean the beets and place them on the baking sheet. Sprinkle the salt over the beets and cover the pan with aluminum foil. Make sure the foil doesn't touch the beets. If necessary, make a little rounded tent above the pan. Roast for 1 hour, or until the beets are tender.

Cool, peel and cut the beets into bite-size pieces.

In a large bowl, toss the beets with the olive oil, pepper, cumin, lemon juice, garlic and parsley. Adjust the seasonings to taste and garnish with more parsley.

The ultimate adopted Israeli breakfast, the roots of shakshuka are Moroccan and Algerian. Israelis came up with their own version, and it is now highly recognized in Israeli cuisine—aromatic, wonderful, healthy and nutritious. Here's my classic version, as I learned it from my mom. We add harissa to our shakshuka for a deep, peppery flavor.

CUMIN SHAKSHUKA

YIELD: 6 SERVINGS

4 tbsp (60 ml) extra-virgin olive oil

4 large red peppers, cut into strips

2 tbsp (10 g) Harissa with Caraway, Cumin and Coriander (page 56) or (30 g) tomato paste

6 large, very ripe tomatoes, chopped

6 oz (168 g) tomato paste

4 cloves garlic, slivered

½ tsp sugar

1 tsp ground cumin

Salt and pepper, to taste

6 large eggs

½ cup (10 g) roughly chopped cilantro

Tahini, for serving

Israeli salad, for serving

Fresh pita, for serving

In a large skillet, heat the oil over medium heat. Once the oil is hot, add the red peppers. Sauté for 10 minutes, or until slightly browned. Add the harissa, tomatoes, tomato paste, garlic, sugar, cumin, salt and black pepper. Stir and bring to a simmer over medium-low heat. Cook for 20 to 30 minutes, or until you have an aromatic, thick sauce. Adjust the seasonings to taste.

Gently break the eggs and pour each into the sauce. Cover the pan and simmer gently for 8 to 10 minutes, or until the egg whites are set but the yolks are still runny.

Remove from the heat, add the cilantro and let the pan rest for a couple of minutes to settle. Spoon onto individual plates and serve with tahini, Israeli salad and fresh pita.

S'chug is a spicy relish or chutney and a favorite condiment for Israeli and Middle Eastern cuisine. It can be super spicy, or you can make it milder. Regardless, it isn't going to taste the same without cumin and cardamom.

CUMIN CARDAMOM YEMENITE S'CHUG

YIELD: 15 SERVINGS

6 jalapeño peppers

3 bunches cilantro leaves with tender stems

12 cloves garlic

1 tsp ground cumin

1 tsp kosher salt, plus more to taste

1 tsp ground green cardamom seeds

1 cup (240 ml) extra-virgin olive oil

In a food processor, combine the jalapeños, cilantro, garlic, cumin, salt and cardamom. Pulse until finely chopped but not creamy.

Transfer to a bowl and slowly stir in the olive oil. Mix well. Taste for salt and add more if necessary. Store in an airtight container in the refrigerator for up to a month.

CHEF'S TIP: Make sure the oil covers the mixture when storing as it will keep it fresh. If you like the recipe and are worried about the level of spiciness, add more cilantro and use less jalapeño. It's just as good but not as hot.

DUKKAH

An Egyptian ground nut and spice blend, dukkah is traditionally served as an amuse-bouche so to speak, with fresh pita and olive oil on the side. Dip the pita into the olive oil and then into the dukkah mix. Let it melt in your mouth as you wait for your main meal.

Dukkah is a rich and fragrant spice mix, adding loads of depth and character to almost any dish. Encrusting fish, lamb or poultry with dukkah or sprinkling it over any sautéed vegetables truly creates a satisfying and addictive dish. You can even nibble on it as a snack all by itself.

The word "dukkah" comes from the Arabic for "to pound," since the mixture of spices and nuts is pounded together after being roasted. These days, dukkah is slowly becoming more popular in countries outside of Egypt. TV chefs in the United States are talking about it and using it on their shows, and it's becoming easier and easier to find, especially online. Once you familiarize yourself with this mix, you'll be using it on everything and dying to share this magical ingredient with your foodie friends.

For the Western palate this is a very exotic and exciting combination of flavors. I encourage you to make your own mix and introduce it to your family and friends. There are many versions and ways to make dukkah, but here's my favorite.

HOMEMADE DUKKAH

YIELD: 1½ CUPS (220 G)

½ cup (70 g) sesame seeds

½ cup (70 g) raw hazelnuts

½ cup (60 g) raw walnuts

2 tsp (4 g) whole cumin

2 tsp (4 g) coriander seeds

Pinch of ground cinnamon

Salt and pepper, to taste

In a large skillet, lightly toast the sesame seeds for 1 to 2 minutes, or until the sesame turns golden and fragrant. Set aside.

In a food processor, place the hazelnuts, walnuts, cumin, coriander, cinnamon, salt and pepper. Pulse until grainy but not powdered. Mix in the toasted sesame. Store in an airtight container, in the refrigerator, for up to 2 months.

CHEF'S TIP: Just like families in Egypt do, I encourage you to create your own mix. Add flavors you love and enjoy, such as roasted sunflower, pine nuts, pumpkin seeds, dried mint, herbes de Provence, nigella seeds, sumac and more. The possibilities are endless!

It is easy to make finger food seasoned with dukkah. Serve on a platter with a little tahini for dipping and you'll have a winning, entertaining bite! Normally, Moroccan cigars are made with a very specific type of filo dough that is not available in the United States, so I substitute it with an easy-to-find wonton dough. The result is just as crispy and crunchy. You can make these cigars with any kind of ground meat or even with mushrooms for vegans.

CRISPY MOROCCAN BEEF AND DUKKAH CIGARS

YIELD: 20 CIGARS

½ cup (120 ml) vegetable oil, divided

1 onion, finely chopped

½ lb (230 g) ground chicken, lamb or beef

2 tsp (4 g) Homemade Dukkah (page 119)

Pinch of ground cinnamon

Salt and pepper, to taste

½ bunch parsley, chopped, plus more for serving

20 wonton wrappers

Tahini sauce, for serving

In a large skillet, heat 2 tablespoons (30 ml) of the oil over medium-high heat. Once the oil is hot, sauté the onion for 10 minutes, or until golden brown. Add the ground meat, dukkah, cinnamon, salt and pepper. Once the meat is cooked through after about 15 minutes, remove from the stove and mix in the parsley.

Place a wonton wrapper on a flat surface and scoop about 1 tablespoon (15 g) of the mixture onto the wrapper. Spread it evenly along one edge, roll up the wrapper to create a cigar-like shape and seal the wrapper with a few drops of water. Repeat with the remaining wrappers.

Heat the remaining 6 tablespoons (90 ml) of oil in the large skillet. Once the oil is hot, pan-fry the cigars, turning on all sides until the cigar is golden and crispy. Serve with chopped parsley and tahini sauce.

This combination of flavors is a perfect complement for duck's gamy, rich flavor. The nutty and aromatic spice mix reveals more layers as you savor the duck.

DUKKAH-CRUSTED DUCK BREAST

YIELD: 2 SERVINGS

2 duck breasts (6–8 oz [168–230 g] each), skin on, at room temperature

Salt and pepper, to taste

4 tbsp (60 ml) extra-virgin olive oil

1 tsp silan (date syrup)

2 tbsp (10 g) Homemade Dukkah (page 119)

Preheat the oven to 375°F (190°C) and line a baking sheet with parchment paper.

Trim the duck breasts of any excess fat and then score the duck's skin every ½ inch (1.3 cm) or so. Make slits in the skin but don't go into the flesh. Pat the breasts dry with paper towels and season with salt and pepper.

Heat the oil in a skillet over medium heat. Once the oil is hot, sear the duck, skin side down, for a few minutes, or until browned and crispy. Flip over and cook the other side for 1 to 2 minutes. Remove the breasts from the skillet and brush the silan on the crispy skin side of the breasts.

Place the dukkah mix on a flat plate and press the duck's skin onto the dukkah to encrust the skin completely.

Place the duck skin side up on the baking sheet and bake for 10 minutes for medium, or longer if you'd like it cooked medium-well.

CHEF'S TIP: I serve this incredibly rich-flavored dish with a simple fresh orange and a purslane or frisée salad tossed in a little bit of olive oil.

Here's a beautiful Middle Eastern–Italian fusion recipe. The dukkah mix will coat the fettucine, adding crunch and flavor in an unexpected way. Once you've made your Homemade Dukkah mix (page 119), this should be easy breezy to prepare.

FETTUCCINE WITH OLIVE OIL, GARLIC AND DUKKAH

YIELD: 4 SERVINGS

1 (16-oz [450-g]) box dried fettucine

4 tbsp (60 ml) extra-virgin olive oil, plus more as needed

3 cloves garlic, slivered

3 tbsp (15 g) Homemade Dukkah (page 119)

Salt and pepper, to taste

¼ tsp red pepper flakes (optional)

2 tbsp (10 g) minced fresh parsley

¼ cup (25 g) freshly grated Parmigiano-Reggiano cheese

Cook the pasta until al dente according to the package directions. Drain the pasta over a bowl and reserve about ½ cup (120 ml) of the cooking water. Set aside.

In a large skillet, heat the oil over medium-high heat. Once the oil is hot, add the garlic and cook until the garlic begins to brown, about 1 minute or less. Stir frequently so the garlic doesn't burn. Stir in the dukkah mix and stir well for 1 minute. If it's too dry, add more oil. Add the salt and pepper to taste and the red pepper flakes (if using).

Add the pasta to the skillet over medium heat and stir in with the dukkah mixture for 1 to 2 minutes. Add the parsley and enough of the cooking water so the pasta is well coated.

Divide the pasta among four plates, sprinkle with Parmigiano-Reggiano and serve alongside a glass of red or white wine.

Salads are a great way to incorporate quinoa, a protein-rich yet almost flavorless seed, into your diet. Even though this salad is served cold, it is still a very comforting and satisfying side or snack. The dukkah adds a certain robustness and nutty flavor that may fill you up before the main course arrives.

QUINOA SALAD WITH DUKKAH, SWEET PEAS AND HERBS

YIELD: 6 SERVINGS

2 cups (340 g) dried quinoa (white, red or rainbow)

4 qt (4 L) water

2 tbsp (30 g) salt, plus more to taste

1 cup (130 g) frozen sweet peas, defrosted

1 bunch asparagus, cut into 1" (2.5-cm) segments

2 tbsp (30 ml) extra-virgin olive oil

2 tbsp (10 g) Homemade Dukkah (page 119)

⅓ cup (15 g) chopped fresh parsley

⅓ cup (30 g) chopped fresh mint

⅓ cup (5 g) chopped fresh cilantro

Zest of 1 lemon

Pepper, to taste

Cook the quinoa according to the package directions. Set aside.

In a medium pot, bring the water to a boil. Add the salt and cook the sweet peas and asparagus for 5 to 7 minutes, or until tender but not mushy. Drain and set aside.

In a large bowl, mix the olive oil, quinoa, cooked vegetables, dukkah, parsley, mint, cilantro and lemon zest, and toss. Add salt and pepper to taste.

CHEF'S TIP: This nutty salad will work with most grilled proteins, so feel free to top with grilled chicken, salmon or steak. Serve it family style or scoop it onto plates.

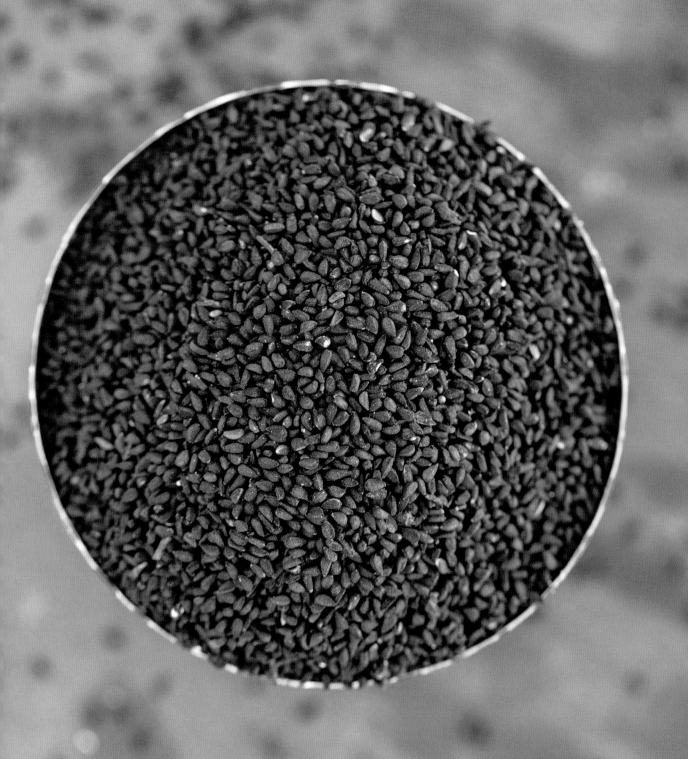

NIGELLA SEED

These tiny seeds have warm-toasted flavors that are perfect for topping soups and sauces. Often mistaken as black sesame, nigella seeds are not sesame at all. Known internationally as onion seeds, black cumin, black caraway, Roman coriander and nutmeg flower, the nigella seed has stood the test of time as a preservative and medicinal agent. In fact, as the story goes, Cleopatra once said that nigella can cure anything but death.

Another story claims that these black seeds were found sprinkled around King Tut's Tomb. Yet another states that the Prophet Muhammad loved the nigella seed for its ability to heal. In more recent times, a woman from Yemen suffering from third-stage cancer claimed to have used nigella seeds as a natural treatment in lieu of Westernized medicine. Three times a day she took the seeds with honey and garlic, and her disease disappeared.

I like to call nigella the spiritual seeds, ones with blessings, and I use them to top fresh-baked bread and salads as well as a vital ingredient in dressings, lamb stew or salmon. Their peppery flavor and mild aroma with hints of onion bring any savory dish to perfection.

No matter the dish you choose, nigella seeds are certain to bring you a spoonful of flavor and health.

This is a fresh salad that's great for outdoor entertaining and can be served individually or family style. The tartness of the labneh (a thick, creamy yogurt cheese) complements the earthiness of the avocado, and the nigella seed adds depth and crunchiness.

AVOCADO, NIGELLA AND LABNEH SUMMER SALAD

YIELD: 4 SERVINGS

½ cup (120 g) labneh

4 cups (80 g) frisée or mixed greens of choice

2 cups (300 g) halved heirloom cherry tomatoes

2 avocados, halved and sliced

4 tbsp (60 ml) extra-virgin olive oil, divided

Salt and pepper, to taste

2 tbsp (8 g) nigella seeds

1 tsp sumac

Seeds from 1 pomegranate (optional)

2–3 fresh mint leaves

Pita chips or lavash bread, for serving

With a tablespoon, scoop the labneh and smear along the bottom of four serving plates. Arrange the frisée over the labneh. Place the tomatoes in between the avocado slices. Sprinkle with 3 tablespoons (45 ml) of the olive oil, salt, pepper, nigella seeds, sumac and pomegranate seeds (if using). Add the mint leaves and finish with a light drizzle of the remaining 1 tablespoon (15 ml) olive oil.

Serve with pita chips or lavash bread.

CHEF'S TIP: Substitute a lemon-infused olive oil for the extra-virgin olive oil for an extra-tart flavor. And if you can't find labneh, you can replace with feta or goat cheese. Or make your own Homemade Za'atar-Spiked Labneh (page 174).

This take on ceviche makes for a perfect appetizer because it's easy to prepare and can be marinated a few hours ahead of time. Unlike South American ceviche, here I combine raw wild fish with lime, orange, mint, nigella seeds and sumac and serve it with pita chips for a no-fuss presentation. The recipe is equally delicious with snapper, corbina or other fresh fillets with a mild flavor.

MEDITERRANEAN SALMON CEVICHE WITH NIGELLA SEEDS

YIELD: 6–8 SERVINGS

1 lb (450 g) skinless salmon, cut into ½" (1.3-cm) cubes

2 tbsp (8 g) nigella seeds, plus more for garnishing

Sumac powder, to taste

Sea salt, to taste

1½ cups (350 ml) fresh lime juice, plus more as needed

½ cup (120 ml) fresh orange juice, plus more as needed

Zest of 1 orange, plus 1 orange slice for garnishing

1 medium red onion, cut into ½" (1.3-cm) pieces

⅓ cup (30 g) chopped mint, plus more for garnishing

35–40 cherry tomatoes

1 fresh jalapeño, sliced (optional)

4 tbsp (60 ml) extra-virgin olive oil

Pita chips or lavash bread, for serving

In a large bowl, mix the salmon, nigella, sumac, salt, lime juice, orange juice, zest and onion. If the fish isn't covered by liquid, add more juice. Mix well.

Refrigerate the mixture for about 4 hours, or until a salmon cube no longer looks raw when broken open. Remove from the refrigerator and add the mint leaves, cherry tomatoes and jalapeño (if using). Mix gently.

Place the ceviche in a large bowl or on individual plates. Garnish with additional mint leaves, nigella seeds and an orange slice. Drizzle the olive oil over the dish and serve with a bowl of pita chips or lavash bread.

Cauliflower steaks are popping up in trendy restaurants, and as much as I like cauliflower, I find that plain grilled pieces of cauliflower are a bit boring. Here, I added a lovely nigella batter to coat these "steaks" and pan-fried them for added texture and depth.

PAN-FRIED CAULIFLOWER STEAK IN NIGELLA SEED BATTER

YIELD: 2–3 SERVINGS

1 large head cauliflower

2 eggs

½ cup (70 g) all-purpose flour

2 tbsp (8 g) nigella seeds

¼ cup (15 g) chopped chives

Salt and pepper, to taste

3 tbsp (45 ml) grapeseed oil

Green salad of choice, for serving

Garlic, turmeric or lemon aioli, for serving

Slice the cauliflower head into 2 or 3 medium-thick steaks. The ends of the cauliflower head won't be good for steaks, so use the center of the cauliflower. The smaller florets can be used as snacks. Set aside.

In a large bowl, combine the eggs, flour, nigella, chives, salt and pepper. Mix until a thick batter forms.

In a medium skillet, warm the grapeseed oil over medium-low heat. Once the oil is warm, dip and cover each cauliflower steak in the batter. Let the excess batter drip and then place the steak in the frying pan.

Fry each side of the steak over low heat for 5 to 7 minutes, or until golden brown on both sides. Be careful not to burn the steaks. You want the batter to be fully cooked on the outside and the cauliflower to be soft inside. Remove from the pan, place on paper towels to absorb any excess oil and serve warm alongside a green salad with aioli.

CHEF'S TIP: I like my cauliflower steak pretty firm so I can cut into it with a knife. If you prefer your steak on the softer side, slice the steaks and then blanch them first in boiling saltwater for 3 to 5 minutes before frying.

This short rib dish is a bit different from your typical recipe. It mixes eggplant, silan, nigella and baharat (page 41) to create an intense flavor. After two hours of simmering, the eggplant magically melts into the sauce and adds thickness and creaminess, while the nigella dots the dish with what seems like pieces of black diamonds.

SHORT RIBS WITH EGGPLANT, SILAN AND NIGELLA SEEDS

YIELD: 4–5 SERVINGS

2 lb (900 g) beef short ribs, cut into individual ribs

Salt and pepper, to taste

1 cup (125 g) white flour

4 tbsp (60 ml) extra-virgin olive oil

1 large onion, diced

4 cloves garlic, slivered

¼ cup (85 g) silan (date syrup)

2 tbsp (8 g) nigella seeds

1 tbsp (5 g) Iraqi Baharat (page 41)

2 cups (360 g) chopped tomatoes

1 eggplant, cut into medium cubes

3 cups (700 ml) water

Season the short ribs with salt and pepper. Then dredge in the flour until coated. Shake off the excess flour.

In a large skillet or Dutch oven, heat the oil over medium-high heat. Place the ribs in the hot oil and cook for 5 to 6 minutes on each side, or until browned. Remove the ribs from the skillet and set aside.

Add the onion to the skillet and brown. Add the garlic and sauté for 2 minutes. Return the ribs to the skillet and mix in the silan, nigella seeds and baharat. Stir well. Stir in the tomatoes and eggplant. Pour in the water to cover the ribs. Cover and simmer over low heat for 2 to 3 hours, or until the ribs are very tender.

CHEF'S TIP: I use this dish as a topping for hummus and serve with fresh pita. The meat melts in your mouth and scooping it with the hummus is pure bliss. Don't forget to sprinkle on some extra nigella for garnishing.

Why serve plain watermelon when you can spice it up?
Easy, fresh and perfect for any summer barbecue, this salad has one of
my all-time favorite harmonies of flavor, crunch and silkiness.

WATERMELON, FETA, NIGELLA AND SUMAC SUMMER SALAD

YIELD: 6 SERVINGS

½ watermelon, cut into large cubes

1 cup (150 g) cubed sheep's milk feta cheese

1 tsp sumac

1 tsp nigella seeds

Zest of 1 lemon

4 tbsp (60 ml) extra-virgin olive oil

Small bunch fresh mint leaves

On a large serving plate, arrange the watermelon and feta cubes. Sprinkle the sumac, nigella seeds and lemon zest over the feta and watermelon. Drizzle with the olive oil and place fresh mint leaves around the plate.

CHEF'S TIP: If you have a hot grill ready to go, try grilling the watermelon slices for 1 to 2 minutes on each side, or until grill marks appear. This will add smokiness to your salad. Simply drizzle a little olive oil on your watermelon and place on a grill.

PAPRIKA

Paprika makes a bold announcement when sprinkled over vegetables or heated in a stew. This ground-up powder, crushed from dried chile peppers or sweet bell peppers, has been dyeing mundane dishes and transforming them into sexy creations since the sixteenth century.

When heated just right, this bodacious spice will release a superb flavor that's sure to stimulate all of the senses, but let's take it back a notch. Where did these delicious little fragments originate and how did they get all the way here into my kitchen?

Christopher Columbus discovered this alluring powder during his travels to the "New World" where the Native Americans used it as a medicinal healing agent. Well, Mr. Columbus was astounded by this mystery powder and returned to Spain with cartloads.

From the sixteenth to the nineteenth century, the demand for paprika grew, with merchants trading this ingredient, from Africa and Asia to Turkey and ultimately to Europe, where it found a welcoming home in Hungary. At first, it was only used to cure fevers, but once the Hungarians realized its culinary capabilities, it became a staple seasoning in their kitchen.

Nowadays, Morocco, Hungary, Poland, Spain, India, South America and California are all major commercial suppliers of paprika. Ranging on the pepper scale from delicate to mild to pungent, and from sweet to hot, the varying types of paprika are incredible. It brings different notes of sweetness or complex notes of heat and, of course, a bright red pigmentation to any dish.

If you can believe it, zookeepers sometimes add paprika to flamingos' food to keep their rosy color. And it's the color that suggests paprika's health benefits. Due to its high beta carotene content, paprika is great for eye health. Beta carotene is converted in the body to vitamin A, which helps the skin rejuvenate and heal.

This dish is traditionally served as a first course every Friday night as it is customary to have a piece of fish during Shabbat dinner. Every family has its own version of it. Tunisians will add harissa and Libyans will add filfel chuma. Some add sliced potatoes and others add chickpeas to the sauce. For the fish, use cod, halibut, corbina, sea bass or even salmon.

NORTH AFRICAN PAPRIKA AND PEPPERS FISH STEW

YIELD: 4 SERVINGS

⅓ cup (80 ml) extra-virgin olive oil

2 red bell peppers, cut into long, thin strips

8 large cloves garlic, coarsely slivered

¼ cup (60 g) tomato paste

1½ cups (350 ml) water

3 large dried red chile peppers (New Mexico pepper works well)

2 tbsp (12 g) sweet paprika

½ tsp ground cumin

1 tbsp (5 g) Harissa with Caraway, Cumin and Coriander (page 56) or filfel chuma (optional)

Salt and pepper, to taste

2 cups (320 g) cooked chickpeas, drained

4 white fish fillets (5–6 oz [140–168 g] each)

Chopped fresh cilantro

Challah bread, for serving

In a large skillet, heat the oil over medium-high heat. Once the oil is hot, add the bell peppers. Let the peppers blister and soften for about 20 minutes. Add the garlic and sauté for 2 minutes. Add the tomato paste and stir well, almost melting the paste into the peppers. Add the water, chile peppers, paprika, cumin, harissa (if using), salt and pepper. Mix well and let the paprika melt into the liquids. Taste and adjust the salt and pepper.

Add the chickpeas and place the fillets in the sauce. Cover and simmer for about 30 minutes, or until the fish is cooked and the sauce is reduced. Turn off the heat and sprinkle with the cilantro. Cover for 5 minutes. Serve with fresh challah bread.

CHEF'S TIP: If you'd like your sauce with a little more spice, replace 1 tablespoon (6 g) of sweet paprika with hot paprika instead.

I love giving classic dishes a spiced interpretation. For schnitzel, adding paprika and sesame to the crust gives it a whole new flavor spectrum. I don't like to pound my schnitzel too thinly, and I love using thighs instead of breasts. It's just so much juicier! You're going to get hooked on this aromatic, juicy chicken cutlet with a crunchy crust that is beautifully reddish and delicious. I promise.

SMOKED PAPRIKA SCHNITZEL

YIELD: 4 SERVINGS

1 cup (125 g) all-purpose flour

2 large eggs

1 tbsp (15 g) Dijon mustard

1 tsp smoked paprika, sweet paprika or both

Salt and pepper, to taste

2–3 tarragon sprigs, chopped (optional)

2 cups (216 g) breadcrumbs or panko

2 tsp (4 g) white sesame seeds

4 boneless, skinless chicken thighs or breasts (5–6 oz [140–168 g] each), pounded to desired thickness

4 tbsp (60 ml) grapeseed oil

Arugula, for serving

Lemon wedges, for serving

Place the flour in a large bowl.

In a medium bowl, whisk together the eggs, Dijon mustard, paprika, salt, pepper and tarragon (if using).

In a large bowl, mix together the breadcrumbs and sesame seeds.

One at a time, dip the chicken pieces in the flour, covering both sides. Shake off any excess flour. Then, dip the chicken pieces into the paprika egg mix and coat evenly. Finally, dip the chicken into the breadcrumbs and sesame, pressing gently to fully encrust the pieces.

In a large skillet, heat the oil over medium heat. Once the oil is hot, brown the chicken for 5 to 6 minutes on both sides. Lower the heat to medium-low heat and cook the chicken through. The crust should be crispy but not burned.

Remove the chicken and place the pieces on a paper towel–lined plate to absorb any excess oil.

Serve it Milanese style with a simple arugula salad and a fresh squeeze of lemon.

Stuffed vegetables are a perfect winter dish served with fluffy rice, tender charred peppers and thick tomato sauce. Everyone likes to stuff peppers with their own creation: yellow rice, red rice, ground beef, ground lamb or a vegetarian creation, but no matter what's inside, baking with sweet peppers is always very satisfying. You can omit the beef here, and it will still be wonderful.

STUFFED SWEET PEPPERS WITH PAPRIKA BEEF RICE

YIELD: 8 SERVINGS

FOR THE FILLING

8 large yellow, red and orange peppers

4 tbsp (60 ml) extra-virgin olive oil

1 red onion, chopped

1 cup (185 g) uncooked jasmine or basmati rice

5 cloves garlic, slivered

1 lb (450 g) ground beef

Salt and pepper, to taste

2 tsp (4 g) sweet paprika or smoked paprika (or 1 tsp of each)

½ tsp cumin

½ cup (70 g) golden raisins

½ cup (60 g) pine nuts

1 cup (240 ml) water, divided

½ cup (20 g) chopped fresh parsley

Preheat the oven to 350°F (175°C). Cut the tops off the peppers and remove the seeds. Reserve the tops and set aside.

To make the filling, in a large skillet, heat the oil over medium heat. Once the oil is hot, sauté the onion for 6 to 8 minutes, or until golden. Add the rice and garlic and cover in the cooked oil. (This prevents the rice from sticking.) Sauté for 5 minutes. Add the ground beef and while stirring and breaking the lumps, add the salt, pepper, paprika, cumin, raisins and pine nuts. Cook for 10 minutes, or until browned.

Add ½ cup (120 ml) of the water. Simmer over low heat for about 10 minutes, or until the rice absorbs some of the liquid. Add the remaining ½ cup (120 ml) water and simmer until the liquid is absorbed. Remove from the heat and stir in the chopped parsley. Let cool and set aside.

FOR THE SAUCE

4 tbsp (60 ml) extra-virgin olive oil

1 yellow onion, diced

6 tomatoes, diced

1 cup (240 ml) water

1 tbsp (15 g) tomato paste

1 jalapeño pepper, chopped and seeded (optional)

Salt and pepper, to taste

½ tsp sugar (optional)

½ bunch cilantro or parsley, chopped

To make the sauce, in a large ovenproof pot (that can fit the peppers), heat the oil over medium heat. Once the oil is hot, sauté the onion for 6 to 8 minutes, or until golden. Add the tomatoes, water, tomato paste, jalapeño (if using), salt and pepper. Bring to a boil and simmer over medium heat for 15 minutes.

Adjust the seasoning. If the sauce is too acidic, add the sugar. Remove from the heat and mix in the chopped cilantro.

Stand the peppers up inside the pot, making sure they can all rest next to each other. Fill the peppers halfway with the rice and beef mixture. The rice will expand and fill up the peppers once fully cooked. Scoop 2 tablespoons (30 ml) of the sauce into each pepper. Cover each pepper with the reserved tops.

Cover the pot with aluminum or its lid. Bake for 30 minutes, or until the rice is tender. Remove the foil or lid and broil for 5 to 10 minutes, or until the peppers are slightly charred. Serve warm with a side salad.

SUMAC

When ground up into a powder, this bold, red spice brings a sultry taste to dishes. Found mostly in the Middle East and the Mediterranean, with a perfume that's reminiscent of summer, sumac is my go-to spice when balancing flavors that need a touch of tang and tart. Although it's not the most popular on America's spice rack yet, it's about ready to take the mainstage, as chefs like myself are preparing unique dishes using sumac as a spotlight flavor.

If you're looking for dishes that are low in salt and high in flavor, sumac is your savior. I recommend it when grilling lamb, topping rice dishes, roasting veggies or cooking fish. Also, keep in mind that sumac does more than add flavor. Its bright burgundy color is a clear sign of high antioxidant content. Like all berries, it's also high in vitamin C.

Here's an extra plus: It may lower blood sugar levels, act as an anti-inflammatory and help with arthritis and skin inflammation. Not too shabby!

This salad always surprises and delights my guests. People are pretty shocked when they realize they're eating raw zucchini. The secret is using thin ribbons of zucchini that are soaked in sumac and lemon and lime juice. Not only does it taste great, it looks amazing!

RAW ZUCCHINI SALAD WITH SUMAC VINAIGRETTE

YIELD: 4 SERVINGS

4–6 medium zucchinis

1 clove garlic, minced

Juice of 2 fresh lemons

Zest of 1 lemon

Juice of 2 fresh limes

2 tsp (4 g) sumac, plus more for garnishing

Salt and pepper, to taste

4 tbsp (60 ml) extra-virgin olive oil

Fresh oregano, mint, dill or tarragon, for garnishing

Roasted pistachios, for garnishing

With a vegetable peeler or a mandoline, cut the zucchinis into strips. Transfer the strips to a large bowl.

In a small bowl, combine the garlic, lemon juice, zest, lime juice, sumac, salt and pepper. Whisk together and thoroughly blend. Drizzle in the olive oil and whisk. When the oil is incorporated, taste to see if you'd like to add some more salt or pepper.

Add the dressing to the zucchini strips and massage to coat. Let it stand for 15 minutes and toss again.

Divide among four salad plates and garnish with fresh oregano, mint, dill or tarragon. You can also add roasted pistachios for some crunch and a dash of sumac.

Seared tuna is usually served in Asian restaurants, but you're about to give it a Middle Eastern twist. The burned salad can be served as is, alongside hummus and fresh pita.

SUMAC AND SESAME-CRUSTED TUNA LOIN WITH BURNED SALAD

YIELD: 2 SERVINGS

FOR THE SEARED TUNA

2 tsp (4 g) sumac

1 cup (140 g) sesame seeds

1 tsp cumin

¼ tsp sweet paprika

Salt and pepper, to taste

2 fresh ahi tuna loins (5–7 oz [140–196 g] each)

4 tbsp (60 ml) avocado oil

FOR THE BURNED SALAD

1 cup (160 g) halved cherry tomatoes

1 jalapeño pepper, seeded and sliced

1 red bell pepper, seeded and sliced

1 yellow bell pepper, seeded and sliced

4 tbsp (60 ml) extra-virgin olive oil, divided

Salt and pepper, to taste

3 cloves garlic, slivered

Juice of 1 lemon

Preheat the oven to 400°F (200°C).

To make the tuna, in a medium bowl, combine the sumac, sesame seeds, cumin, paprika, salt and pepper. Transfer to a flat sheet pan or plate.

Brush the tuna loins with the avocado oil. Place a loin on top of the spice mix and press down. Flip and press down again. Repeat with the other loin. Heat a large skillet over high heat. When the pan is very hot, add the tuna and sear on each side for 2 to 3 minutes. The tuna should be served rare. Chill the tuna in the refrigerator.

To make the salad, place the tomatoes and peppers on a baking sheet, skin side up. Drizzle 2 tablespoons (30 ml) of the olive oil over the vegetables, add salt and pepper and roast for 15 minutes. Turn the oven to broil and cook for 5 minutes, or until the skins are nicely torched.

Remove the vegetables from the oven, transfer to a bowl, cover with plastic wrap and let rest for 20 minutes. This will help separate the skins from the vegetables if you care to peel the vegetables before serving. (You can try it either way without sacrificing taste!) Place them on a cutting board, and chop them into medium chunks for a rustic salad.

Place the vegetables in a bowl. Add the garlic, remaining 2 tablespoons (30 ml) olive oil and the lemon juice, and season with more salt and pepper.

Place the salad on two plates. Cut the chilled tuna into medium slices and place on top of the salad.

What is fattoush? Think of it as the equivalent of the Italian panzanella. In the Middle East we toast old, dry pita with olive oil, and add salt and either sumac or za'atar. This creates a crunchy dimension to an otherwise ordinary salad. This pairs nicely with grilled fish or meat.

SUMAC-SPICED FATTOUSH SALAD

YIELD: 6–8 SERVINGS

FOR THE DRESSING

4 tsp (8 g) sumac

¾ cup (180 ml) extra-virgin olive oil

Juice of 2 lemons

Salt and pepper, to taste

FOR THE SALAD

2 stale (a day old or so) pita breads, sliced

4 tbsp (60 ml) extra-virgin olive oil

Salt and pepper, to taste

Sumac, to taste

3–4 medium tomatoes, quartered

5 English cucumbers, cut into medium-thick slices

4 scallions, thinly sliced

1 small head romaine lettuce, chopped crosswise into medium-thin strips

2 cups (80 g) fresh Italian parsley leaves, plus more for garnishing

1 cup (90 g) fresh mint leaves, plus more for garnishing

Sheep's milk feta (optional)

Preheat the oven to 350°F (175°C).

To make the dressing, in a medium bowl, add the sumac, olive oil, lemon juice, salt and pepper. Whisk until combined. Set aside.

To make the salad, brush the pita bread slices with the olive oil. Sprinkle the salt, pepper and sumac over the pita. Place on a baking sheet and toast for 15 minutes, or until golden brown and crunchy. Remove the pita from the oven and let them cool. Break the slices into uneven medium pieces and set aside.

In a serving bowl, mix the tomatoes, cucumbers, scallions, lettuce, parsley and mint. Drizzle the dressing over the salad. Toss well until evenly coated.

Top the salad with the feta cheese (if using) and the pita pieces. Finish with a few more mint and parsley leaves and serve.

My childhood peanut butter and jelly sandwich was raw tahini and silan on a fresh-baked pita. I took the memories of my go-to sandwich and created this very healthy crowd-pleasing gem. Vegan and packed with a nutritious base with exotic toppings, this is a perfect brunch side dish that will leave your palate in wonder.

SWEET POTATOES WITH SUMAC AND SILAN-INFUSED TAHINI SERVED WITH HERB POMEGRANATE SALAD

YIELD: 4 SERVINGS

4 sweet potatoes

1 cup (220 g) raw tahini

½ cup (170 g) silan (date syrup) or maple syrup

1 tbsp (5 g) sumac

1 bunch fresh parsley leaves

1 bunch fresh mint leaves

Seeds from 1 pomegranate

4 tbsp (60 ml) extra-virgin olive oil

Salt and pepper, to taste

Preheat the oven to 400°F (200°C).

Wash the sweet potatoes (don't peel them) and place them on a baking sheet. Poke holes in the potatoes with a fork and cook for 30 to 45 minutes, or until the skin is charred and the flesh is tender. Remove from the oven and set aside.

In a medium bowl, mix the tahini, silan and sumac until combined. Set aside.

In a separate medium bowl, mix the parsley, mint, pomegranate seeds, olive oil, salt and pepper.

Cut a lengthwise slit in each sweet potato. Don't cut all the way through so they stay intact. Place each potato on a serving plate and generously drizzle with the tahini. Top each potato with the herb salad and serve.

CHEF'S TIP: Sweet potatoes can also be sliced prior to cooking and served by pouring the sauce over them and finishing it off with the salad. You can also place the same ingredients into a food processor and create a sweet potato tahini mousse served with a side of the herb salad and fresh pita.

TURMERIC

Turmeric is the main medicine man. At least that's what the ancient Greeks thought, and if you don't believe them, take Marco Polo's word for it.

From its amber color and earthy texture to its unique medicinal properties, it's easy to see why this golden-yellow powder righteously earned the title of the spice that heals. Known as the anti-inflammatory spice, turmeric is one of the most scientifically researched spices to date—with a history that goes back thousands of years. Not only does it bring color and flavor to a bowl of white rice, but it actually acts as a one-stop shop for your medicine cabinet.

A natural antiseptic and antibacterial agent, liver detoxifier, painkiller and COX-2 inhibitor, it feels like there's nothing this herb can't fix. If your detective eyes are looking for answers, look no further than its most active property, curcumin. This magical compound can help with weight management and some research suggests that it can reduce the risk of childhood leukemia. The health benefits are endless, and it's so potent, that some will isolate it from the root and eat it by itself as a remedy.

If you're looking for a new spice to cook with, dash in a daily dose of turmeric. It's just what the doctor ordered.

Let's combine two of my favorite things: crispy-yet-tender potatoes and turmeric, the super spice! What's not to like? On a side note, here's a thought: Kids love potatoes, so this is a secret way to have your kids consume and develop appreciation for the turmeric flavor.

CRISPY TURMERIC-ROASTED POTATOES

YIELD: 6 SERVINGS

4 tbsp (60 ml) grapeseed oil, divided

1 red onion, chopped

4 cloves garlic, sliced

2 lb (900 g) Yukon gold potatoes, halved

½ tsp turmeric powder, or more if desired

1 tsp kosher salt or lemon salt, plus more to taste

½ tsp freshly ground black pepper, plus more to taste

2–3 fresh thyme stems

Fresh parsley, chopped, for garnishing

Preheat the oven to 375°F (190°C). Drizzle a baking pan with 1 tablespoon (15 ml) of the grapeseed oil.

In a large bowl, combine the onion, garlic, potatoes, turmeric, salt, pepper, thyme and remaining 3 tablespoons (45 ml) of grapeseed oil. Mix until the potatoes are well coated.

Pour the potatoes onto the baking pan and bake, tossing occasionally, for 30 to 35 minutes, or until the potatoes are tender on the inside and beautifully browned on the outside. Sprinkle with the parsley and adjust the salt and pepper to taste before serving.

This book is a love song to my family, and this recipe is one of my favorite memories of my grandmother Rachel. Grandma Rachel used to make this soup once a year, only after Yom Kippur to break the fast. All of the uncles, aunts, cousins, brothers and sisters would gather at her tiny apartment and wait for this fragrant soup as the first course after fasting for the last 24 hours. This delicious soup made it worth the wait. My mom and I continue to break our Yom Kippur fast with this recipe.

TURMERIC AND CILANTRO CHICKEN SOUP

YIELD: 6–8 SERVINGS

4–6 qt (4–6 L) water

1 chicken (2½–3 lb [1.1–1.4 kg]), washed with only excess skin removed

3 large yellow onions, diced

3 cloves garlic, minced

1 tbsp (6 g) turmeric powder

1 tbsp (15 g) organic chicken bouillon

Salt and pepper, to taste

1 large bunch fresh cilantro, whole leaf with stems removed

1 tbsp (5 g) Harissa with Caraway, Cumin and Coriander (page 56) (optional)

1 (16-oz [450-g]) box thin egg noodles, cooked (optional)

In a large, 6-quart (6-L) pot, add the water, chicken and onions. Cover the pot and bring to a boil. Simmer for 1 hour over medium heat, and skim the water for excess fat.

Add the garlic, turmeric, chicken bouillon, salt and pepper and simmer for 1 hour over medium-low heat, or until the chicken is very tender.

Remove the pot from the heat and mix in the cilantro and harissa (if using).

If using noodles, place a small amount on the bottom of each soup bowl. Pour the soup over the noodles and serve.

CHEF'S TIP: There are a few secrets to the heavenly flavors of this comforting soup, including the generous amount of onion, the slow cooking time, the cilantro and, of course, the harissa mixed into the soup right before serving it!

My mom, my aunts, Grandma Rachel and my daughter's Grandma Jackie all cook different versions of this dish, and they all are crowd-pleasers! No matter who we cook it for, Israelis or Americans, Middle Easterners or Anglos, this dish is super fragrant and super tasty. As I write this, I wish I had it in front of me. Although it's painted with turmeric, the addition of cumin makes this a standout side dish on any table.

TURMERIC BASMATI RICE WITH RED LENTIL KITCHRI

YIELD: 6–8 SERVINGS

½ cup (120 ml) canola oil, or more as needed

1 onion, diced

8 cloves garlic, thinly sliced

2 cups (370 g) uncooked basmati rice, rinsed and drained

2 cups (385 g) orange lentils, rinsed and drained

4 cups (1 L) water

2 tsp (4 g) ground cumin

2 tsp (4 g) turmeric powder

2 tsp (4 g) ground coriander

Salt and pepper, to taste

1 tbsp (5 g) caraway or cumin seeds, for garnishing

In a medium saucepan, heat the oil over medium-high heat. Once the oil is hot, add the onion and sauté for 6 to 8 minutes, or until golden brown. Add the garlic and simmer for 1 minute. Don't let the garlic burn! Add the rice and lentils and sauté over low heat for 8 minutes, or until fully covered in oil.

Add the water, cumin, turmeric, coriander, salt and pepper. Stir well and bring to a boil. Reduce the heat and cover tightly with the lid. (In my family we put a kitchen towel over the lid to make sure we lock all the steam inside as it helps to cook the rice.) Cook for 20 minutes. Turn off the heat and let it stand with the lid on for another 15 minutes. Do not open the lid as the heat and moisture will escape.

Transfer the kitchri to a serving dish and sprinkle with caraway or cumin seeds.

Cauliflower is finally becoming more popular in American cuisine. It is healthy, delicious, versatile and beautiful. This recipe produces a gorgeous side dish that deserves to be a star on any dinner table. In addition, this is what I'd like to call easy, breezy, lemon squeezy! Simple to make, delicious to taste, healthy to no end!

TURMERIC-ROASTED CAULIFLOWER

YIELD: 2–4 SERVINGS

6 qt (6 L) water

2 tbsp (12 g) turmeric

3 tbsp (45 g) salt, plus more to taste

1 head cauliflower

4 tbsp (60 ml) extra-virgin olive oil

Pepper, to taste

2 or more thyme sprigs (optional)

Labneh, for serving (optional)

Preheat the oven to 450°F (230°C).

In a large pot, bring the water, turmeric and salt to a boil. Reduce the heat and carefully add the whole cauliflower. Simmer for 15 to 20 minutes, or until the cauliflower is tender but not falling apart.

Place the cauliflower on a baking sheet, drizzle the olive oil over it, sprinkle with the pepper and thyme (if using) and bake for 10 to 15 minutes, or until the top of the cauliflower is lightly charred. Remove from the oven and place on a serving plate. Serve with a scoop of labneh, if desired.

My whole family loves pickles. Grandma Rachel pickled anything from garlic to watermelon peels. Her recipes had turmeric in them, so the pickles would be beautifully yellow, and they were served with nearly every meal on a side platter. Below is a quick brine recipe and all the variations you can play with. I received this recipe from my dear friend Aria Kagan, whose cooking I truly respect.

SPICED PICKLED VEGETABLES

YIELD: 16 OZ (475 ML)

2 cups (475 ml) water

4 tbsp (60 g) Celtic salt

½ cup (100 g) sugar

1½ cups (350 ml) white vinegar or raw apple cider

Cucumbers, green tomatoes, okra, carrots, cabbage, etc. (or a mixture of all)

In a large pot, add the water, salt, sugar and white vinegar. Bring the water to a soft boil. Simmer over medium-low heat for 15 minutes, or until everything has been fully dissolved.

Now choose the veggies to be pickled and the spice mix (see options below).

In a mason jar, add the spice mixture and then fill the jar with your vegetables all the way to the top. Feel free to squeeze them in as they will lose some volume. Pour the brine all the way to the top and seal well. Mix and shake and dance with the jar. Let the jar stand until it cools down and then place in the refrigerator for at least 24 hours.

Enjoy alone or as a vibrant condiment to any of the dishes in this book.

SPICE MIXTURES TO ADD TO THE BRINE

OPTION 1
2 tsp (4 g) mustard seeds

½ tsp turmeric

2 tsp (4 g) celery seeds

1 onion, sliced

2 tsp (4 g) fennel seeds

1 tsp cumin seeds

1 tsp coriander seeds

OPTION 2
1" (2.5 cm) chopped ginger

5 cloves garlic, sliced

1 tbsp (6 g) sesame seeds

½ tsp turmeric

1 bunch scallions, chopped

OPTION 3
2 jalapeño peppers, minced and seeded, if desired

2 tsp (4 g) cumin seeds

1 tsp coriander seeds

½ bunch cilantro, chopped

OPTION 4
2 tsp (4 g) caraway seeds

2 tsp (4 g) brown mustard seeds

1 tsp red pepper flakes

3 dill sprigs

ZA'ATAR

Za'atar, Arabic for the word "thyme," is a blend of thyme, sumac, toasted sesame seeds and wild oregano. Israelis aren't the only cooks in the kitchen using this precious combo. It actually dates back to the Middle Ages. But those advocates actually saw it as a medicinal agent instead of a cooking ingredient and used it to help regulate moods and sleep cycles, improve memory and fight cancer. The Jewish philosopher and physician Maimonides (1135–1204) even prescribed it to his patients. And if you ask today's scientists, they'll say those historical remedies have truth to them.

Better known in present-day Middle East as a brain booster, there are scientific studies that show za'atar to improve cognition. And even more so, its main ingredients are natural antioxidants that help protect human cells from damage as well as release serotonin. So, if you're looking to increase your children's test scores, do as those in the Middle East do and dust your morning pita toast (lightly dipped in olive oil) with a spoonful of za'atar. Meanwhile, I also highly recommend using it to spice up your cooking! Rubbed on homemade labneh, chickpeas, lambchops and even popcorn, this titillating jumble of herbs will bring an ounce of zizz and zazz to any of your home-cooked recipes. And you can even make it yourself! Simply add equal parts of dried, coarsely ground hyssop (or thyme if you can't find it); toasted sesame seeds; sumac (optional) and salt (to taste).

This is a fun, healthy snack that the whole family will enjoy. Chickpeas are full of fiber, minerals and protein. I make mine with a kick, but feel free to omit the chili powder and use sweet or smoked paprika only.

CRUNCHY ZA´ATAR CHICKPEAS

YIELD: 8–10 SERVINGS

4 tbsp (24 g) za'atar

Salt and pepper, to taste

1 tsp smoked or sweet paprika

1 tsp chili powder

4 cups (640 g) chickpeas, soaked overnight, drained

2 tbsp (30 ml) extra-virgin olive oil

Heat the oven to 375°F (190°C). Line a baking sheet with parchment paper.

In a small bowl, mix together the za'atar, salt, pepper, paprika and chili powder.

Spread the chickpeas on the baking sheet. Drizzle the olive oil over the chickpeas and then dust with half of the spice mix. Bake for about 30 minutes, stirring occasionally to make sure the chickpeas are evenly roasted.

Place the hot chickpeas in a bowl and sprinkle with the other half of the spice mix and serve.

CHEF´S TIP: Serve this either hot or cold with a glass of wine, a cold beer or the beverage of your choice. For extra crunch, you may deep fry the chickpeas and then mix in with spices.

This is one of my all-time favorite homemade cheeses, especially if made from sheep or goat's milk. Drizzled with za'atar and olive oil and served with fresh pita or crusty country bread, it is an irresistible combination for me. Labneh is not easy to find, but yogurt is, and it's super easy to make labneh from yogurt at home.

HOMEMADE ZA'ATAR-SPIKED LABNEH

YIELD: 4 SERVINGS

17 oz (478 g) plain full-fat yogurt (sheep's milk is ideal, but regular full-fat yogurt will work as well)

½ tsp salt

2 tbsp (12 g) za'atar, plus more for serving

1 cheesecloth bag with string

1 tsp extra-virgin olive oil, plus more for serving

Rosemary (optional)

Red pepper flakes (optional)

In a medium bowl, add the yogurt, salt and za'atar. Mix well.

Pour the yogurt mixture into the cheesecloth bag. Tie the bag. Hang the cheesecloth over a big water pitcher using a knife or chopstick. Place the pitcher in the refrigerator at least overnight. You'll see the liquid from the yogurt slowly dripping down to the bottom of the pitcher. Make sure the bottom of the cloth is hanging and not touching the bottom of the pitcher.

The cheese can be left for 1 to 2 days, until the desired consistency is reached. The longer the cheese is left, the firmer it becomes. If you'd like spreadable labneh, 1 day is more than enough to wait. For labneh "balls," let it sit refrigerated for 2 days. Then form the balls and store in an airtight container with olive oil, rosemary (if using) and red pepper flakes (if using).

Remove the labneh from the cloth and transfer to a covered container. Drizzle the olive oil on the cheese to keep it fresh longer. To serve over a salad, scoop the cheese and drizzle olive oil and extra za'atar.

CHEF'S TIP: In addition to the za'atar, you can mix or match other spices, such as coriander, sumac, whole or ground cumin seeds or dried chile peppers. Lemon or orange zest or fresh herbs such as parsley, mint, dill or cilantro can add delicious flavor as well.

By now I assume you have read that microwave popcorn is a big no-no for optimal health. It is regarded as very unhealthy due to the chemicals added to the bag. In addition, many families choose not to cook with a microwave at all. So let's have some fun and make popcorn the old-fashioned way.

ZA'ATAR COCONUT POPCORN

YIELD: 6–8 SERVINGS

2 tbsp (30 ml) melted coconut oil

½ cup (100 g) popcorn kernels

¼ tsp salt

2 tsp (4 g) za'atar

In a tall pot, heat the oil, covered, over medium heat. Once the oil is hot, add the popcorn kernels and cover. Shake to ensure all the popcorn kernels are covered in the oil. Once there is a pause of more than 5 seconds between pops, turn off the stove and remove the popcorn from the heat. Let it sit for a few minutes.

Pour the popcorn into a large bowl. Add the salt and za'atar, and combine well. Eat it hot and fresh!

CHEF'S TIP: Feel free to explore other flavors, such as sumac, caraway seeds, smoked paprika, cumin, freshly ground black pepper, Parmigiano-Reggiano, dried parsley or even a cinnamon and brown sugar mix.

If you're a lamb lover and you've never tasted a lamb and za'atar combo, you're in for a treat! This recipe is easy to follow, delicious and beautiful to behold on the table.

ZA'ATAR-CRUSTED RACK OF LAMB

YIELD: 3–4 SERVINGS

1 cup (110 g) breadcrumbs

½ cup (48 g) za'atar

Zest of 1 lemon

2 tbsp (30 ml) extra-virgin olive oil, plus more as needed

2 lamb rack cutlets, each with 4–5 chops (1 lb [450 g] each)

Salt and pepper, to taste

Preheat the oven to 375°F (190°C). Lightly oil a baking pan.

On a large, flat plate, mix together the breadcrumbs, za'atar and lemon zest.

In a large skillet, heat the oil over medium-high heat. Once the oil is hot, sear the lamb for a few minutes on the outside. Sprinkle with salt and pepper as you sear them. The searing will help the crust stick to the rack once it's in the oven.

Dip each rack into the breadcrumb za'atar mix until fully crusted. If necessary, brush extra oil on the racks.

Place the racks on the baking pan and roast for 15 to 20 minutes for medium rare or longer for desired doneness.

CHEF'S TIP: While working on the racks, you can separately roast potatoes or root vegetables to serve alongside the lamb.

This recipe will change your life. This bread is virtually carb-free, filled with healthy fats and calcium and packed with protein. If you are on a low-carb diet, this bread will be perfect for you. Plus, it only takes 20 minutes to bake!

ZA´ATAR-SCENTED CARB-FREE TAHINI BREAD

YIELD: 1 LOAF

4 large eggs

5 tbsp (75 g) raw tahini

2 tbsp (40 g) raw honey

1 tsp baking powder

Salt, as desired

1 tbsp (5 g) za'atar, plus more for garnishing

Preheat the oven to 350°F (175°C).

In a large bowl, mix together the eggs, tahini, honey, baking powder, salt and za'atar. Stir really well. Pour the mix into a greased loaf pan. Sprinkle more za'atar on top for garnishing.

Bake for 20 minutes, or until golden brown on the outside and a toothpick inserted into the center comes out clean and dry. Let it cool off before serving.

CHEF'S TIP: I love slicing a piece of this bread and spreading almond milk cream cheese on top. Also, you can make a sweet version of this by adding cinnamon and raisins instead of za'atar.

Focaccia is traditionally Italian, but here I've given it a Middle Eastern twist using za'atar and olives. This is absolutely wonderful for dipping or snacking.

ZA'ATAR AND OLIVE FOCACCIA

YIELD: 4–6 SERVINGS

¾ cup (180 ml) warm water, divided, plus more as needed

½ oz (14 g) dry active yeast

1½ cups (190 g) all-purpose flour, plus more as needed

1 tsp table salt

½ cup (90 g) pitted and quartered black olives

2 tbsp (30 ml) extra-virgin olive oil, plus more as needed

1 tbsp (5 g) za'atar

2 pinches of coarse sea salt

Preheat the oven to 425°F (220°C). Lightly oil a baking sheet.

In a small bowl, place ½ cup (120 ml) of the warm water and stir in the yeast. Let it sit for 10 minutes, or until frothy.

In a large bowl, sieve the flour and salt and then with a wooden spoon, stir in the yeast mixture and the remaining ¼ cup (60 ml) water. If the dough is not elastic enough or feels dry, you might need to add a little more water.

Transfer the dough to a floured surface. Knead for 15 minutes by hand or 7 to 10 minutes by machine until smooth and elastic. Place the dough in a well-oiled bowl, cover with plastic wrap and set aside in a warm place to proof for 1½ hours, or until doubled in size.

Turn the dough onto a floured surface, punch down, and then sprinkle in the olives and knead for about 3 minutes, until the olives are fully incorporated throughout the dough. You might need to add the olives in two batches.

Place the dough on the baking sheet, pulling it into a rectangle about ¾ inch (2 cm) deep.

Make dimples in the dough using your fingers, and then brush the olive oil over the surface. Sprinkle on the za'atar and sea salt. Bake for 15 to 20 minutes, or until golden. Serve warm or at room temperature with olive oil for dipping.

RESOURCES

AMAZON

By now you know you can find pretty much anything on Amazon.com, and there are some Middle Eastern vendors that will ship you herbs and spices quickly. Don't forget to read the sellers' reviews.

www.amazon.com

SADAF

This site features condiments, dried fruit, beans, pickles, sauces and more.

www.sadaf.com

THE SPICE AND TEA EXCHANGE

This Florida-based company with stores throughout the US features quality products and wonderful customer service. They also have great online shopping tools and will ship almost anywhere.

www.spiceandtea.com

GLOSSARY

BULGUR is sometimes confused with cracked wheat, which is crushed wheat grain that has not been parboiled. But bulgur is actually cracked wheat that has been partially cooked. So soaking the fine-grind variety in hot water for 10 to 15 minutes makes it soft enough to consume in salads, such as tabbouleh, or to form into a dough. A distinction is made between fine-ground bulgur and a coarser grind. It is defined by grind sizes (#1 fine, #2 medium, #3 coarse and #4 extra coarse).

FILFEL CHUMA literally means "peppers and garlic" and is the typical hot condiment of Libyan Jewish cuisine. It comes from Libya, where it is known as masser. It is a thick paste made from powdered sweet and hot paprika, vegetable oil, salt and minced garlic.

HARISSA is a North African hot chile pepper paste, the main ingredients of which are dried red peppers soaked in water for a few hours, spices and herbs, such as garlic paste, coriander seed or caraway, as well as some vegetable or olive oil for preservation. Harissa is most closely associated with Tunisia but is also common in Libya and Morocco. We mix it in sauces, soups and stews, and serve it as a condiment during meals.

HAWAIJ is the name given to a variety of two Yemenite ground-spice mixtures. One is primarily used for soups and the other is called hawaij and is for coffee. Hawaij has been used extensively by Yemenite Jews in Israel, and its use has spread more widely into Israeli cuisine as a result. The basic mixture for soup is used in stews, curry-style dishes, rice and vegetable dishes and even as a barbecue rub. It is made from cumin, black pepper, turmeric and cardamom. More elaborate versions may include ground cloves, caraway, nutmeg, saffron, coriander, fenugreek and ground-dried onions. The mixture for coffee is made from aniseeds, fennel seeds, ginger and cardamom. Although it is primarily used in brewing coffee, it is also used in desserts, cookies and cakes.

ORANGE FLOWER WATER OR ORANGE BLOSSOM WATER is the clear, perfumed water that is a by-product of the distillation of fresh bitter orange blossoms for their essential oil. It is very fragrant and has traditionally been used in many Middle Eastern desserts to enhance flavor. Orange flower water has found its way to many cultures and cuisines: in France to flavor madeleines, in Mexico to flavor little wedding cakes and in the United States to make orange blossom scones and marshmallows. It is also used as an ingredient in some cocktails, such as the Ramos Gin Fizz. In Malta and many North African as well as Middle Eastern countries, orange blossom water is widely used as medicine for stomachaches.

S'CHUG is a hot sauce originating in Yemenite cuisine. Peppers, garlic and cumin are the base, but each family or region has its own version. You can make red or green s'chug, depending on the color of hot pepper you're using. Some add cilantro for a milder, more aromatic taste. Always serve hummus with some type of s'chug on the side!

SEMOLINA FLOUR is the coarse, purified wheat middlings of durum wheat mainly used in the Middle East for making couscous. (Sometimes it comes with a number next to it for grain size: go for #2.)

SILAN is a thick, dark and sweet syrup extracted from dates. It is widely used in North African and Middle Eastern cooking. In the Middle East, we mix it with raw tahini and spread it on bread for breakfast. I also use it on sweet potatoes. Yum! Use it as a dip for bread, in pastries and as a topping for assorted desserts and mousses.

TABIL is an Algerian and Tunisian spice mixture generally consisting of ground cumin, coriander seed and caraway seed. Traditional harissa is always spiced with tabil. Other ingredients might also be included based on personal preference, such as rose powder, garlic powder or cloves. The term can also refer to coriander by itself.

ACKNOWLEDGMENTS

I would like to thank a few people who made this book possible: Renée Sayegh for surrounding me with love and light. Thank you for going over every word of this book with so much love and wisdom. Caren Glassman for your support and encouragement. Nicole Schubert for your never-ending enthusiasm. Thank you for sprinkling some of your spicy words throughout this book. Valerie Lopez and Camilo Rojas, your friendship shines like a diamond. Sonja Garnitschnig, your soul filled the photography from the day The Spice Detective became a reality. Chef Jose Pinot of Shiraz Creative for working with me on countless events over the years and for your insight into some recipe creations. Shai Tertner and Jason Harder and the entire Shiraz Creative family, for always believing in me. Special thanks to The Spice and Tea Exchange for providing me with quality spices and herbs from around the world. A huge thank you to Page Street for making this book a reality. And to my daughter, Rachel, who inspires me every day to be the best person I can be. You're the greatest gift, and you fill my life with meaning.

ABOUT THE AUTHOR

YANIV COHEN is the vice president and culinary director of the award-winning catering, design and production company, Shiraz Creative. Nestled in the kitchen as an infant and encouraged to cook as a child, he quickly developed a huge passion for food, along with an increasing fascination with the medicinal properties of food, herbs and spices.

In 2014, Yaniv started a blog and YouTube channel called The Spice Detective, where he shares his love for food, spices, herbs and well-being with the world. In 2018, The Spice Detective collaborated with St. Roch Market to open JAFFA, an outlet for his spice-centered cuisine within the Miami Design District's distinguished food hall. Some highlights include a hummus bar, deconstructed baba ghanoush and assorted grilled meats.

To view original Spice Detective videos and learn more about spices and herbs and their flavors, aromas, properties and health benefits, please visit: thespicedetective.com.

INDEX